FUNDAMENTAL STRATEGIES FOR

REAL ESTATE

INVESTING

FUNDAMENTAL STRATEGIES FOR

REAL ESTATE INVESTING

KENNETH K. BOTWE

Books By Ken: Available on Amazon.com

Dedication

This book is dedicated to everyone who wants to build wealth through real estate investing. Your chances of succeeding is greatly elevated through preparation.

TABLE OF CONTENTS

INTRODUCTION

ALLOW ME TO welcome you to **Fundamental Strategies for Real Estate Investing**. My name is Ken Botwe, and I'm the director of education at DeviseWealth.com and Devise Wealth Mastermind Facebook Group. I'm also the author of several books such as **5 Principles for Becoming Wealthy, Little Money Big Credit, Pursuit of ~~Happiness~~ Assets, Nurture** and this one as well. You can find all my books on amazon.com.

I'm also a United States Air Force Veteran and a serial entrepreneur with an ample amount of experience in real estate. With a professional background in business and finance, I have established and continue to operate several businesses, real estate, and investments in the stock market. My passion is helping people just like you, who want to quickly get out of bad debt, establish great credit, pay off your house and build wealth with real estate, business, and investments so you can enjoy life every day.

I began this journey helping my family, friends, and others in my community who reached out to me. I was perfectly ok with that, but one day a friend of mine confronted me and basically called me selfish. I was confused and immediately demanded an explanation because I'm the least selfish person you'll ever meet. He said, you are successful and have a vast amount of experience and knowledge, right? I said yes, then he went on and asked, why aren't you sharing this information with a lot more people? I replied, haven't I taught you many things in the area of personal finance and wealth building? In fact, haven't I done the same with all our family and friends for that matter? He said yes, and what percentage is that compared to everyone you could help?

I paused and thought about it; then he said you have to share your knowledge with the world.

He was right. My knowledge and experience should be used to serve more than just my immediate circle, but how do I know if people wanted my insightful experience? To find out, I decided to take a survey. It turns out people do want to learn but don't know where to start. Knowing this, I began to make plans. My mission evolved from working with a selected few to helping the masses in the area of wealth building. Real estate is, by far, the most sustainable tool because volatility has no presence in this industry.

A mere conversation that occurred over 15 years ago led me to a series of actions such as publishing books, courses, articles, training videos, one on one coaching, and becoming a director of education at my companies. I enjoy helping people; that's why I pledged to teach wealth building to everyone that's willing to learn. One of my favorite ways of building wealth is through real estate investing. As you read the chapters that follow, you'll see why I'm so elated about fundamental strategies for real estate investing.

CHAPTER 1

WEALTH BUILDING WITH REAL ESTATE

Many individuals around the country often tell me that they want to invest in real estate, yet many do not seem to take any real action. Their reasons, I've come to learn are a result of not having the capital to get started, not knowing where to start and the fear of losing money. These are all valid concerns for those who aren't exposed to or haven't learned the best strategies for real estate investing.

In my e-book, 5 Principles for becoming wealthy, I wrote about the importance of the learning principle. When you have the proper knowledge, none of the above-mentioned excuses will be relevant. They are limited beliefs designed for those who don't know. This is why I emphasize the need to learn before engaging in any investment or venture.

For instance, people that have spent the time educating themselves already know that you can invest in this business without any money. They further understand that specialized knowledge can be used creatively in the absence of money, especially when the burning desire is present.

It is a fact that knowledge is just as valuable as money in the real estate industry if you can utilize and leverage it well.

There are three major ways to make money with real estate as illustrated in the graph below. When my students start with no or little money, I teach them to spend 50% of their efforts in doing wholesale deals. The reason is due to the fact that it can be done with minimal resources. What's more important is the skill required to do it correctly. Fix and flip takes 30% of the efforts because there's a great opportunity of earning substantial amount per transaction. In other words, a person that does rehabbing can sell and walk away with a larger check. Rental income properties gives the owner a continuous cash flow. It is a matter of doing the work once and getting paid over and over. Of course, there will be maintenance after a few years especially if you rehab before renting.

As you can see, each area of real estate has it benefits therefore the ability to do all three is paramount. You can employ a strategy of saving capital from wholesaling and then use it for rehabbing. Some of the proceeds from fix and flip can be used to secure rental income properties which can build your long-term net worth among others.

3 Ways to Make Money with Real Estate

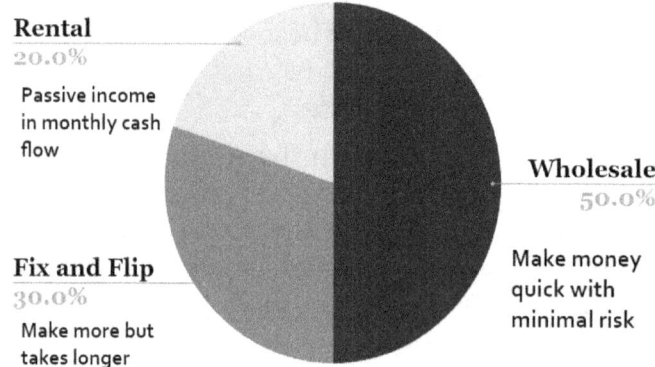

Rental
20.0%
Passive income
in monthly cash
flow

Wholesale
50.0%
Make money
quick with
minimal risk

Fix and Flip
30.0%
Make more but
takes longer

As for not knowing where to start, it is a matter of your level of understanding and choice. What one new investor may deem as an appropriate start often varies. It comes down to goal and personal preference once the process is clear. I know folks that started very bold and went after large acquisitions. These people, for the most part, had partners with multiple years of experience. On the other hand, the individuals who started with caution often gain confidence fairly quickly after a few deals and feel as if they can move on to bigger properties.

The fear of losing money is real. It must be mitigated through education and properly conducting due diligence. Not knowing can be costly to a point where a new investor may lose confidence and exit the real estate business. Additional problems occur when people learn the bare minimum and proceed without any solid guidance.

My solution for all these potential issues is a systematic approach through this publication. In the chapters that follows, I have laid out complete and best strategies that even a beginner can follow to begin acquiring wealth through real estate investing. You have a choice on where to start because I've broken down the systems into three main categories. Read and master them all and then decide which one is most appropriate for a start.

There are multiple ways to build wealth. Some take the route of acquiring wealth through business. This can probably be the most profitable, but it does require a lot more capital, the right type of business, and proven systems. Another venue that people choose is stock market investing. It too can produce significant capital gains when stocks are sold or traded, but there's no control of market turns. Real estate, on the other hand, is stable, and historically, we've seen a steady increase in appreciation. This means that the value continues to rise and therefore, your equity at the time of purchase only grows bigger.

Since nothing is guaranteed, the knowledge to evaluate the market and utilize it for decision making is indispensable. Let's say you want to purchase a property that cost $200K. Knowing how to assess using essential tools such as sales comparable, inspection, appraisal, and repair estimate are all great, but it doesn't tell you what tomorrow holds for that local market. In the event the market goes crazy, and the value diminishes over a one-year period, a knowledgeable real estate investor would have no worries.

We'll cover three different strategies for investing in real estate. Of the three, the one that a local market downturn applies to is the buy and hold through renting income properties. We'll cover this extensively in later chapters. The other two strategies which will be covered later as well but doesn't apply because you will not hold the property for an extended period. The subject will become more evident when we reach later chapters that covers the other strategies. Either way, an experience investor will come out on top.

They would have already taken the correct measure in their calculus of the property before purchasing, therefore, minimizing even a volatile market which, as I stated, is quite unusual for real estate.

You see, to protect yourself against a local market downturn, as a result of jobs moving out of the area or other issues, an experienced investor would make sure they don't pay more than the replacement cost of the property. There are many ways to get access to this information, including asking your insurance agent or builders in your local market.

If the replacement cost for the $200K property is only $150K, you have overpaid in terms of market downturn. In other words, you want the replacement cost to be the same or higher than what you paid. This strategy ensures that a builder is not able to build a similar house at a cheaper market rate than your property. Failing to pay attention to this factor or simply not knowing can cause problems for those that buy and hold. By doing considering this cost to build as well as the other modes of evaluation, you can rest assured that you are purchasing your long-term properties using complete and the best strategies.

Wealth in real estate come in several fashions with each having its advantages and disadvantages. A person who may not have the capital to get started can learn the specialized knowledge required to perform real estate wholesaling.

With this method, you are not buying the property. You are merely getting the property under contract and assigning the contract to other investors. This strategy and others will be covered extensively through the coming chapters.

CHAPTER 2

STRUCTURE YOUR BUSINESS PROPERLY

Before you start your real estate business, you must take care to structure it properly. I will provide examples of documents that will help your business; however, any contracts or agreements should be reviewed or revised by your attorney to ensure compliance with state and local laws. That said, any substantial asset should be treated like a business. Whether it's business itself, real estate, or investment, take the time to structure it properly.

To protect your assets, you must have a clear legal distinction between you and your assets. For instance, you own some personal things such as a house, a car, or other valuables and have decided to start wholesaling. Your first action should be to incorporate your business. By doing so, the business stands on its own.

If any issues arise outside of the real estate business, no one can successfully go after your house, car, or other valuables in a lawsuit. Without the articles of formation in a Limited Liability Company (LLC) or Incorporation (C-Corp or S-Corp), a plaintiff can win judgment order on anything that you own. By forming a legal entity like an LLC or a Corporation, you have legally separated yourself from your business entity and therefore protected your assets.

It is worth to note that in America, some state has franchise tax law. If your state has it, you'll have to file franchise tax each year for your corporation or LLC. For most states, as long as your business earns less than $250,000, you are not required to pay a franchise tax. Whether you meet that threshold or not, you'll have to file every year. In such a case, you'll file a zero due.

By law, you must file for a federal employer identification number or FEIN if you live in the United States. There are similar requirements in other countries, but for the US, you can attain it online. Visit www.IRS.gov to apply. They will issue a letter assigning you a FEIN which will be a series of numbers that will be used to identify your business and determine your tax liability. Once assigned, you'll file a tax return annually whether you generate income or not.

At some point when money begins to accumulate through your wholesale business efforts, it would serve you well to add an experienced and reputable accountant and a lawyer to your professional team. Each has its duties in preparing documents and providing solid advice to help your business. Your job is to make deals, and you'll get very good at doing this if you focus strictly on that and let the mentioned professional handle the accounting and legal stuff.

Asset protection serves many more purposes. Besides the legal separation between you and your assets, purchasing insurance is another form of asset protection. When you have adequate insurance, any loss or damage would be covered, therefore preserving your assets. Insuring your assets works the same way as your auto and home except it is called General Liability Insurance or GL insurance. When the unforeseen occurs, the insurance company will pay, and your asset will remain intact. There's no logical reason not to insure valuable assets.

Same things apply to intellectual properties such as trademark, systems, and things of that nature. These assets can be plagiarized or stolen, but having asset protection means your attorney can take legal action to correct violators. There is no shortage of violators, so protecting your assets serves as a deterrent and thieves ultimately go where there are no protections in place.

As you can see, the need for a sound mindset in asset protection is very important when you have things of value. Simple precaution and a little investment for safeguarding your assets will save you from unnecessary loss in the litigious society of today.

Although you can incorporate your business yourself, it is advisable to pay an attorney in your state to file the documents for you. I make this assertion because there may be some unforeseen things that you may miss if you do it yourself. Besides incorporating, there are other requirements such as operating agreements, certificates of shares, initial minutes, annual meetings, etc. and not adequately meeting the requirement means your vulnerability.

In other words, your corporate veil can be pierced. You are going to accumulate material wealth, therefore, assemble a substantial legal castle to protect yourself. You can wait until you do your first few deals and invest some of the proceeds to protect yourself and your business properly.

Setup a home office when you first start, and you can eventually move to a professional office space as your business grows. Although most of the work can be done on your smartphone, you should have a real home office setup with items such as desk and chair, computer, printer, internet, and stationery. Image is everything, so give your business a professional name and logo and create marketing material. We'll go deeper into all of this through this book.

Another major part of structuring your business is installing systems and processes that will enable you to work on your business more than working in your business. Don't be afraid to use these systems to delegate duties and responsibilities to your personal assistant and others a so you can focus on what brings in the money. If you adopt the mentality of doing it all by yourself, you'll do yourself a major disservice. Think about it.

You are just one person and are limited in what you can do but a team will enable you to accomplish much more.

Tools and software can also help you get more done with less.

It is very important that you either develop these documentations of systems and processes or purchase them. Having a system for instance for talking to seller for instance ensures that even if you are away, your assistant or other team member can do that assignment. They can do these types of things and you can suddenly come in and close the deals.

CHAPTER 3

BUILD A TEAM

A leader has to assemble a team that not only believes in the vision but embodies it. Although the leader sets the agenda, it is the manager that carries it out.

This is why it's extremely important to have a clear vision and mission when you are a leader of any group. In real estate, a team is valuable because they determine the extent of your long-term success.

These professionals consist of realtors, loan officers, mortgage brokers, title companies, contractors, insurance agents, property managers, lawyers, and accountants.

As your partners, they make your transactions from start to finish smooth. The skill and insight they bring to the table simply cannot be substituted.

Get yourself an experienced mentor that has enjoyed a level of success. Since they've been there, their advice is reliable and will help you cut the learning curve. People often feel as if this step can be skipped, but I assure having someone who has already reached the heights you wish to attain is indispensable. By heeding to this wisdom, you'll avoid so many potential pitfalls and relatively stay on course more fluently.

Lending is one of the smartest ways to secure funds needed to acquire an asset. Some conditions must be met for banks and other lenders to give you money. Banks and creditors like for borrowers to have "skin in the game," meaning they will usually require you to have a down payment of your loan amount. It's still better than having to raise the total capital on your own. All of that is understood, but the efficiency of accessing money when needed is depended on having a relationship with a couple of loan officers and private money lenders. It may be the difference between closing a deal quickly and losing it.

Regardless of the type of real estate investment, you decide to pursue, having a few good contractors in your back pocket is highly advised. Imagine having a motivated seller ready to sell well under market value. All you need is for a contractor to give you an estimate of the cost of repairs so you can make an offer.

With contractors on your team, this is an easy task. Without it means you'll have to either find one or wait for an inspector to come out in a few days to determine what needs to be repaired. Even then, they can't give you an estimate. Their job is to tell you what's wrong, not the cost to repair. As you can see, a contractor would help speed up the process immensely.

Contractors can save you a lot of time and money while inspectors can uncover the extent of repairs needed. Insurance agents are also valuable in many ways. Besides the usual of providing an estimated cost to insure a property, they can reveal the total replacement cost of a property. This value is especially important when there are concerns of a market downturn.

Deals are closed with the assistance of a title company. These title agents handle documents, check records and officiate closing between buyers, sellers, and wholesalers. The wholesaler that invest in the business and equip it with skillful staff will outperform those who don't possess the same. As your business grows, be sure to re-invest in it.

This exercise includes adding staff such as an assistant who can prescreen, visit, and evaluate properties before turning it over to you.

The need for more staff with different duties will arise as your business grows.

Top professional has the staff support and systems necessary to provide a great experience one transaction at a time. To increase this frequency, it is good to assemble in-house staff as opposed to outsourcing. It really depends on your plans. Do you want to grow fast, or are you ok with just a few transactions a month. If you want to grow fast, you'll have to use your team as well as automate every possible aspect of the business.

Again, your business efficiency depends on how well you are able to get things done automatically and with minimum effort from you. Finding deals and qualifying them certainly can all be automated so you can focus on the relatively more important aspect of your real estate

Business. A rule of thumb is to focus on all things money and have the team do all the things that leads up to the money.

CHAPTER 4

TOOLS AND RESOURCES

Aside from formulating a strong team for your real estate business, there are tools that you must have at your disposal to make the business function optimally. The first one is a website that clearly states your core business. This site must have lead capture so you can collect seller and buyer leads for follow-up. Investing in a good website these days doesn't cost much, and the return on investment is enormous. To capture leads, your unique selling proposition or USP has to grab potential client's attention, or you can just offer valuable information in exchange for your prospects contact email and telephone number.

A beginner doesn't really need to invest a lot of money into a deal flow app. Instead, you can use some of the free and relatively cheap methods that I'll disclose in chapter 6. As you begin to make deals and earn money from real estate, you will then naturally scale up by investing in a more rapid and deal flow such as apps that gives you access to all the potential motivated sellers in your market of interest.

Combing through these apps can be time-consuming, but you'll be able to afford a personal assistant by that time to filter and contact leads.

When you identify a property, you must know how to properly evaluate it before making an offer. There are many ways to do it, but the most important is through the use of sales comparable. This tool can be accessed through websites like Trulia and Zillow; however, the most accurate and complete information is available through a multiple listing service. A great and mutually beneficial relationship with a realtor is advised because they'll get you the comps that you need. Some may even give you access by making you their associate if the relationship warrants it.

Staying within the scope of tools and resources, you'll also need a repair estimate tool of some sort. It can be as simple as a form that lists all the parts and cost of a house or more detailed as a deal analyzer spreadsheet or app. What toll you use is a matter of preference because all of them does basically the same thing. The end result is knowing what repairs are needed and the cost in material and labor to do so.

Equally as important is a way to manage your prospects and customers. Again you can set up a customer relationship management systems via spreadsheet at the beginning, but as your business grows, you'll be better served with a CRM system that allows automation and setting of reminders. Either way, you'll be able to build and nurture relationships of your prospect and customers.

There are so many forms, scripts, and sample contracts that will help your business operate smoothly, and all of them will be provided at the end of this publication for your reference. Forms such as lead intake and document such as contract to purchase are just a few of the tolls that every serious real estate investor must have and utilize. Even knowing what to say when you contact your leads can be confusing for a beginner, so I've provided a sample of that as well. There's no need to overwhelm yourself when you first start with complex systems. It is more practical to keep everything simple and focused on making deals and gaining experience.

If your real estate investment company requires using a contractor, there are forms and contracts that will keep them honest and reliable. Not knowing about these tools could be a lot of unforeseen trouble down the line. Throughout the years, I have perfected how to get the most out of my contractors and hold their feet to the fire. The tools I use and all the stipulations I make will be thoroughly discussed in chapter 9, so you can handle contractors with confidence.

Even the real estate investor that sells or rent properties must take certain measures to ensure quick transactions for profit or cash flow. Everything from knowing how to price the house to staging it properly and professional photos are all essential resources. For instance, placing and changing lockbox combination after contractor work is completed, and access is given to real estate agents for showing can save you time.

A properly executed contract will ensure that your best interest is protected during transactions. Contingency clauses will serve those purposes, so you are not blind-sided at any point during the process due diligence and beyond. The more you do deals; you'll develop your own unique set of essential tools that simplifies things to your liking. Examples of tool, forms, and resources we use are attached for your reference.

The first is a seller lead sheet, and details of it is explained in chapter 7. The process of beginning to acquire a wholesale property includes finding out about the property and its owner. The seller lead form will capture relevant information for that purpose. Fannie Mae Homestyle renovation Mortgage provides a loan for rehab. The terms are usually better than the hard money lender. See the attached sheet and find more about their current rates on their website. Next, there's a script for returning calls and setting appointments. More on this subject as well as explanation is found in chapter 7 as well.

Property repair estimate is an integral part of real estate due diligence and knowing how to accurately identify what needs repairs is essential. You also need to know how to estimate the material and labor cost of these repairs. The attached repair and estimate form will help you evaluate the property so you can make an offer.

It has an estimated cost for each item already included but be sure to double check with local home building warehouse for current ongoing prices in your area.

When you have a completed lead intake and repair estimate, you'll seek sales comparable from the MLS through a real estate agent as discussed in chapter 7 and 8. Through the use of these resources, you can adequately evaluate the property and make an offer. When the offer is accepted, you'll put the property under contract using a document called contract to purchase. A copy is attached, but your attorney should provide or revise it to comply with local laws and fit your agreement.

Once the property is under contract, you can do further due diligence such as inspection, appraisal, scope of work and estimated repair cost, etc. depending on the extent of your investment. A wholesaler will not have to do many of these things a rehabber will. More on each strategy will be covered throughout this publication. For wholesalers, you'll assign the property to an investor for a profit with a document sample attached called agreement to assign contract for sale and purchase.

Samples of yard signs are provided. Before utilizing this effective tool, check local ordinances to ensure that it's permissible in your area to avoid fines or removal. The exception is placing a sign on your yard. The signs are very effective in dense shopping areas and events centers.

Your business should be professional and organized. The first impression is a lasting one so assemble a buyer's folder to include at a minimum, the things listed in the attached sample. You'll assign or sell to these investor buyers over and over again if you choose wholesaling. Leave a folder with each of them after an encounter even if they don't buy the first time.

The next three forms are lien waiver and release forms. These documents will help you avoid a lot of issues with contractors if you rehab houses. Through the use of these forms, a contractor that signs them can't come back later and put a lien on your property. The final one is signed once the work is completed and all payments have been made.

There are a serious of responsibilities business owners have. Among them are those that contract work. In this case, a W-9 must be completed when you first contract a job so that you can provide a from1099-Misc to your contractor for tax purpose since they are not classified as your employee. Those that are your employees, however, must complete a W-4, and you'll provide them with a W-2 at the end of the year.

Keep in mind that it costs a lot more to have an employee than a contractor, but some rules needs to be followed for each. For example, you must withhold income tax, social security, and Medicare from wages paid to an employee while the contractor is responsible for their own. In a nutshell, if they are trained by you and can resign at any time, then they are an employee. However, a contractor has a business license, can make profit or loss and does the same work for multiple people.

Income tax and matching social security and Medicare withheld is paid quarterly via form 941, also attached. Various types of form 1120 are used to file a corporation's tax return. Your tax accountant can help you not only choose the correct form based on your business setup but save you money in allowed deductions. Make sure you use an accountant that specializes in real estate. Some states are required to file franchise tax so be sure to check to avoid forfeiture. Real estate purchase, lease, and rental agreement should definitely be provided by an agent or an attorney to ensure compliance and your protection. A sample of eviction notice is attached.

SELLER LEAD SHEET

Contact Person: _____ Prop/Title Owner _____

Property Address: _____

City: _____ State: _____ ZIP: _____

Cell Phone Number: _____ Email: _____

Vacant?_____ House / Condo / Other _____

What are you looking to sell the property for _____ Is that flexible _____

Mortgage Balance $_____ Monthly Pymt: $_____

Mortgage Interest Rate: _____ % PITI? _____

Are you current on payments _____ Months Behind _____ Amount Behind _____

Back taxes _____ Other Lien Amounts _____

If I can do the deal quickly, what's the best you can do _____

How did you come up with Asking Price:_____

Why are you selling?_____

What repairs are needed?_____

When do you want to move?_____

Bedroom: _____ Bathroom:_____ Half Bath:_____

Square Feet:_____ Lot Size:_____ Sq. Ft. / Acre(s)

Construction: Brick?   Hardie plank?   Stucco?   Other_____

Garage: 1   2   3   +   Carport:_____ Basement:_____

Refrigerator:_____ Range:_____ Dishwasher: _____

Have you discussed selling your house with someone else? _____ What about a realtor _____

Notes:

_____

_____

_____

_____

_____

Internal Office Information Only

Appointment date_____ Time_____ Evaluator

_____

After Repair Value _____ As Is Value_____ Repair cost _____ Offer _____

Borrowers now have an easy and affordable option to finance home renovations.

HomeStyle Renovation is a conventional mortgage that lets borrowers finance improvements, renovations or repairs to a home at the time of purchase or as a refinance transaction—up to 75% of the as-completed appraised value of the property.*

Flexible

Purchase or refinance option for any renovation project such as design updates or improvements, and even renovating accessory units like in-law suites or basement apartments.

Affordable

Your borrowers can take advantage of competitive rates, which may be lower than a home equity line of credit (HELOC) or a personal loan.

Simple

Standard pricing and conventional execution. Loans can be delivered even before the project starts and eligible for R&W relief once completed.

(Conditions apply)

Bundle mortgage products for more flexibility and savings

Both HomeStyle Renovation and HomeStyle Energy mortgages may be combined with a HomeReady® mortgage, so your low- to moderate-income borrowers can take advantage of the following features

- Low down payment and cancellable mortgage insurance (restrictions apply)
- Potentially lower rates than other forms of financing such as home equity line of credit or credit cards
- SPECIAL PRICING – Get a $500 LLPA credit when combined with the HomeStyle Energy product on energy upgrades (no energy report required for certain projects)

To become an approved HomeStyle Renovation lender, submit **form 1000A** to your Relationship Manager.

We've simplified and expanded eligibility for HomeStyle Renovation.

	New HomeStyle Renovation	Government Rehab Loan
Maximum LTV (1-unit owner-occupied)	Up to 97% (See Fannie Mae's Eligibility Matrix for specific details based on the loan transaction)	96.5% x Up to 110% of the "as-completed" value
Minimum / maximum renovation costs	For Purchase: Limited to 75%* of the lesser of the purchase price plus renovation costs, or the "as-completed" appraised value. For Refinance: Limited to 75% of the "as-completed" appraised value	Standard 203(k) Minimum cost = $5,000 Limited 203(k) Maximum cost = $35,000
Can be used on ANY project	✓	✗ Eligible projects are explicitly listed; prohibited projects are explicitly listed. Eligibility varies based on 203(k) Standard or Limited
Can finance accessory units (e.g. in-law suites, basement apartments, etc.)	✓	✓ Standard 203(k) ✗ Limited 203(k)
Applicable to manufactured homes	✓ No structural changes allowed	✓
Allows upfront draws	✓ Up to 50% of material costs	✓ Up to 50% of material costs
Includes contingency reserve / allowance	✓ Up to 15%	✓ Up to 20%
Easy loan delivery	✓ Conventional pricing / execution. Special approval required for loans delivered before renovation is completed.	✗ Requires FHA / GNMA approval
Rep. & warrant relief eligibility	✓ Once renovation is completed (Subject to standard Selling Guide requirements on R&W relief)	✗ No R&W relief available
Can use ANY contractor / subcontractor for project	✓ Contractors must be licensed only when required by state law	✗ Contractors must be licensed per state / local requirement. 203(k) approved consultants must be used
Requires proof of completion	✓ Form 1004D only	Letter of Completion and Final Release Notice
Allows servicing transfers	✓ When work is complete	✗ No explicit policy
Guidelines on delinquency	Loan must be current at the time of recourse removal, with no more than one 30 day delinquency during the renovation period.	Project extensions may only be granted if borrower is current. Lender may refuse to make further draws if mortgage is delinquent; project must cease if mortgage is in default.

FAQs

Can lenders use HomeStyle Renovation financing on a manufactured home?

Yes, manufactured housing is eligible for HomeStyle Renovation financing, up to the lesser of 50% of the as-completed value, or $50,000. The manufactured home must meet the applicable Selling Guide requirements in Section B2-3-02, Special Property Eligibility and Underwriting Considerations: Factory-Built Housing.

Can an accessory unit be detached from the primary dwelling?

Yes, an accessory unit may be detached from the primary dwelling. All improvements related to accessory units must be in compliance with local and state codes and statutes. They also must meet the applicable Selling Guide requirements for accessory units in Section B4-1.3-05, Improvements Section of the Appraisal Report.

Can landscaping costs be covered?

Yes, provided that the improvements are permanently affixed to the property.

Is an energy report required when using HomeStyle Renovation for energy-related improvements?

It depends on how the transaction is structured as well as the types of energy improvements completed. If energy-related improvements are financed through the HomeStyle Renovation product without using HomeStyle Energy, an energy report is not required. In that case, the lender will not deliver the loan with Special Feature Code 375 and will not receive the $500 loan-level price adjustment (LLPA) credit.

When combining HomeStyle Renovation with HomeStyle Energy, lenders will receive the $500 LLPA credit if Special Feature Code 375 is delivered. The transaction will also be subject to the requirements under HomeStyle Energy when this option is used. Some improvements under HomeStyle Energy require the borrower to obtain an energy report while others do not. For additional information about when energy reports are required for HomeStyle Energy loans, see Selling Guide section B5-3.3-01, HomeStyle Energy for Energy Improvements on Existing Properties.

Script for Returning Calls and Setting Appointment

This is (Your name) with (Your company), returning your call. How may I help you? After listening to their desire to sell their property, you'll begin by confirming their full name. Proceed by telling them about your company and what you do. You can say something like this: **Our Company lifts the burden of mortgage, taxes, repair, and risk of bad credit off people. We can help you get out of unpleasant situation and you don't have to pay 6% commission to a realtor.** If you have a minute, I would like to ask a few questions so I can make you an offer. When they consent, go ahead and ask the questions on the intake form and write down their responses. Say thank you, we'll do an evaluation and call you back with an offer, Bye for now.

This is (Your name) again with (Your company), we are almost ready to make you an offer. We'll just need to do a site visit of your property and then we can make the offer. Will 9am on Saturday work for you? If not what day and time? Write down the date and time and say: We'll see you then, Thanks bye

Street Address: _____ Date: __/__/__ Inspected by: _____
City: _____ ( ) Occupied ( ) Vacant
Beds: ____ Baths: ____ Sq. Ft. ____ Year Built: ____

Property Repair Estimate Sheet

Inspection Checklist	Yes	No	Unknown	Unit	Repair Cost Calculations	Repair Cost
1. Chimney Need Repair/Replacement?					Repoint $500 Rebuild $1,000-$5,000	
2. Roof Need Repair/Replacement?					(Single): $5,000-$8,000 $275-$350/Square (100 sq. ft.)	
3. Exterior Paint/Siding Need Repair/Replacement?					Paint: Sing. Fam. 1500 sq. ft.: $3,000-$5,000 Siding (Single Family): $6,000-$8,000 $275-$500/square	
4. Windows Need Repair/Replacement?					# of Window x $325-$500 Bay Window: $1,000-$2,000 Repair $25-$100	
5. Exterior Doors Need Repair/Replacement?					$250-$400 ea.	
6. Garage Need Repair/Replacement?					1 Garage Door: $650 1 Reframe Structure: $1,500 1 Car Int. Paint: $500 2 Car Int. Paint:$1000	
7. Driveway Need Repair/Replacement?					$2,500-$5,000 average driveway replacement $4-$6/sq. ft.	
8. Yard cleaned/landscaped?					Landscape $300-$5,000	
9. Fence Need Repair/Replacement?					$100-$150/section	
10. Septic Need Repair/Replacement?					$5,000-$20,000	
11. Heating or furnaces Need Repair/Replacement?					Replace 1 Furnace: $3,000 Replace 1 Boiler: $4,000 Replace 1 Hot Water Heater: $800-$1,200 Install 1-2 Zone Baseboard Heater Including Boiler: $7,000-$10,000 FHW	
12. Plumbing Need Repair/Replacement?					$1,000-$5,000 Rough Plumbing (drains, venting, water lines, etc...) $800-$1,500 per fixture (i.e. laundry hook-up, sink, etc...)	
13. Electrical Need Repair/Replacement?					1 New Panel: $1,000-$1,500 Fixtures: $400-$1,000 1 New Service, Panel, Rewire House: $5,000-$10,000	
14. Foundation Need Repair/Replacement?					$50-$150/linear foot	
15. Basement structure Need Repair/Replacement?					Pour Concrete Floor: $1-$3/sq. ft. (new) $0.50-$6/sq. ft. (repairs) Replace Stairwell: $1000-$2000 Lally Column $100-$200 LVL $10-$20/linear	
16. Interior Doors Need Repair/Replacement					$125-$200 ea.	
17. Closet Shelving					$50-$100 per closet	
18. Framing Need Repair/Replacement					$500-$5,000 depending on scope	
19. Interior Trim Need Repair/Replacement					$2-$4/linear foot	

20. Need interior paint?				Interior Paint: $2 a sq. ft. (living space) as a general rule Single Family: 1500 sq. ft. $2800	
21. House need carpet?				Carpet $2-$4/sq. ft.	
22. House need laminate/vinyl?				Laminate/vinyl $3-$6/sq. ft.	
23. House need tile?				$5-$10/sq. ft.	
24. Floors need to be sanded/installed				Hardwood Install = $6.00-$10 sq./ft. Sand & Refinish= $1.25-$2 sq./ft.	
25. Kitchen Cabinets Need				Single Family Cabinets and Counters: $2,500-$6,500	
26. Insulation need replacement?				Attic/Basement: $1-$1.50/sq. ft. Wall: $0.50-$1/sq. ft. (coverage area)	
27. Kitchen - need appliances?				1 Stove: $500-$1,000 1 Refrigerator: $800-$1,500 1 Overhead Microwave: $300-$500 1 Dishwasher: $350-$700	
28. Bath Fixtures/accessories?				Shower: $600-$2,000 Install add: $500 Toilet: $75-$200 Install add: $150 Vanity/Sink: $150-$600 Install add:$300 Mirror/Towel Bar/Toilet Paper Holder/Towel Ring: $100-$300	
29. Sheetrock Need Repair/Replacement?				Patches: $1-$2/sq. ft. Skim Coat Only: $0.50-$1/sq. ft. New Blueboard/Plaster/Drywall: $1.10-$1.50/sq. ft.	
30. Dumpsters/Demo?				Dumpsters: $500 ea. Demo Labor: $500/filled dumpster	
31. Decks?				Decks: 10x10 = $2,000 15x15= $3,000	
32. Other:_____					
33. Miscellaneous				Repair Cost x .10%	
34. Comments:_____				Total Repair Cost:	$.

After Repair Value	
ARV X 75% $.	
(Subtract Repairs) $.	
Maximum Offer $.	

Heating System: Boiler   Furnace

Heating Fuel: Gas   Oil

In Ground Oil Tank: Yes   No

Water: City   Well

Sewer: City   Septic

28

REAL ESTATE CONTRACT TO PURCHASE

THIS AGREEMENT MADE THIS _____ DAY OF _____,_____ BY AND BETWEEN
_____, SELLER AND _____, BUYER. SETTLEMENT SHALL
TAKE PLACE WITHIN_____ BUSINESS DAYS, OR ON_____. THIS AGREEMENT IS
SUBJECT TO AND CONTINGENT UPON BUYER INSPECTION AND BUYER OBTAINING
FINANCING. BUYER WILL HAVE IMMEDIATE RIGHT OF ENTRY AND THE RIGHT OF
POSSESSION FOR OBTAINING ESTIMATES FROM GENERAL CONTRACTORS, SHOWING
PARTNERS/ASSIGNEES AND GENERAL INFORMATIONAL AND INSPECTION PURPOSES.
SELLER AUTHORIZES THE BUYER TO MARKET THE PROPERTY FOR RESALE OR LEASE
TO ACCOMPLISH FINANCIAL GOALS PRIOR TO SETTLEMENT. THIS PROPERTY IS BEING
SOLD IN ITS " AS IS ". SELLER DOES HEREBY SELL AND CONVEY UNTO BUYER AND
BUYER DOES HEREBY PURCHASE FROM SELLER, THE REAL PROPERTY KNOWN AS
_____ INCLUDING ALL IMPROVEMENTS,
APPURTENANCES, RIGHTS, PRIVILEGES, EASEMENTS, AND OTHER PROPERTY
INTERESTS EXISTING THEREON. BUYER WILL PAY_____
DOLLARS(_____) OF WHICH _____(_____) HELD AS A REFUNDABLE
DEPOSIT HAS BEEN PAID IN CASH AT THE SIGNING HEREOF TO BE HELD BY _____
UNTIL CLOSING WITH THE BALANCE OF THE PURCHASE PRICE TO BE PAID AT
SETTLEMENT. AT SETTLEMENT, UPON PAYMENT AS ABOVE, PROVIDED OF THE UNPAID
PURCHASE MONEY, A DEED AND FURTHER ASSURANCE WILL BE EXECUTED BY THE
SELLER TO CONVEY PROPERTY AND ALL INTERESTS THEREIN TO BUYER. TITTLE WILL
BE GOOD AND MERCHANTABLE, FREE AND CLEAR OF LIENS AND ENCUMBRANCES. IF
SELLER IS UNABLE TO CONVEY TITLE FREE AND CLEAR OF LIENS AND
ENCUMBRANCES THE DEPOSIT WILL BE RETURNED TO THE BUYER. _____ WILL
PAY ALL TRANSFER COSTS. SELLER WILL CURE AT THEIR OWN EXPENSE ANY
OUTSTANDING LIENS, ENCUMBRANCES, OR JUDGMENTS. IF THE SELLER DEFAULTS
UNDER THE TERMS OF THIS CONTRACT, BUYER MAY PURSUE ALL REMEDIES
AVAILABLE AT LAW OR AT EQUITY INCLUDING COLLECTION OF MONETARY DAMAGES
AND/OR SPECIFIC PERFORMANCE OF THIS CONTRACT. IF THE BUYER DEFAULTS,
SELLER MAY HAVE THE RIGHT TO MARKET THE PROPERTY. THE PARTIES HERETO
BIND THEMSELVES, THEIR HEIRS, PERSONAL REPRESENTATIVES, SUCCESSORS, AND
ASSIGNS FOR THE FAITHFUL PERFORMANCE OF THIS CONTRACT.

SELLER:_____ DATE: _____

BUYER: _____ DATE: _____

AGREEMENT TO ASSIGN CONTRACT FOR SALE AND PURCHASE

SUBJECT PROPERTY:

LEGALDESCRIPTION:

THIS AGREEMENT IS MADE BETWEEN _____ (ASSIGNOR)
AND _____ (ASSIGNEE) REGARDING PURCHASE OF ABOVE
REFERENCED SUBJECT PROPERTY. WHEREAS_____ (BUYER)
HAS ENTERED INTO A PURCHASE AND SALES AGREEMENT
WITH _____ (SELLER) FOR THE PURCHASE OF SUBJECT
PROPERTY, AND WHEREAS BUYER WISHES TO ASSIGN ITS RIGHTS, INTERESTS
AND OBLIGATIONS IN THE PURCHASE AND SALES AGREEMENT, IT IS HEREBY
AGREED BETWEEN ASSIGNOR AND ASSIGNEE AS FOLLOWS:

1. THE TOTAL ASSIGNEMENT FEE DUE TO ASSIGNOR WHEN ASSIGNEE CLOSES
WITH SELLER IS _____DOLLARS(_____)

2. ASSIGNEE SHALL PAY ASSIGNOR A NON-REFUNDABLE DEPOSIT OF
_____DOLLARS(_____) PAYABLE WITH SIGNING
OF THIS CONTRACT

3. ASSIGNEE SHALL PAY ASSIGNOR A NON-REFUNDABLE ASSIGNMENT FEE OF
_____DOLLARS(_____) MINUS THE DEPOSIT OF
_____DOLLARS(_____) PAYABLE AT CLOSING

ASSIGNEE:_____ DATE: _____

ASSIGNOR: _____ DATE: _____

WE BUY HOUSES

FAST CASH & AS-IS

000-000-0000

WE BUY HOUSES

CASH ANY CONDITION

000-000-0000

HOUSE FOR RENT

3-2 NEWLY RENOVATED

000-000-0000

HOUSE FOR RENT

3-2 NEWLY RENOVATED

000-000-0000

HOUSE FOR SALE

3-2 NEEDS TLC 50K

000-000-0000

HOUSE FOR SALE

3-2 NEEDS REPAIR

000-000-0000

Wholesale Folder for Buyers

SECTION 1

Your company logo and contact information
Street view photo of property
Property address
Any special features

SECTION 2

Contents

SECTION 3

County tax/appraisal records

SECTION 4

Detail property description

SECTION 5

Remaining photos and short video of inside and outside property & street view

SECTION 6

After Repair Value or ARV

Sales comparable for 3 to 4 similar properties

Comparative Market Analysis or CMA

SECTION 7

Estimated repair sheet

SECTION 8

Resources for the buyer such as Lender, Contractor, Title Company and Real estate agent

NOTICE:
This document waives rights unconditionally and states that you have been paid for giving up those rights. It is prohibited for a person to require you to sign this document if you have not been paid the payment amount set forth below. If you have not been paid, use a conditional release form.

UNCONDITIONAL WAIVER AND RELEASE ON PROGRESS PAYMENT

Project _____

Job No. _____

　　The signer of this document has been paid and has received a progress payment in the sum of $_____ for all labor, services, equipment, or materials furnished to the property or to _____ (person with whom signer contracted) on the property of _____ (owner) located at _____ _____ (location) to the following extent: _____ (job description). The signer therefore waives and releases any mechanic's lien right, any right arising from a payment bond that complies with a state or federal statute, any common law payment bond right, any claim for payment, and any rights under any similar ordinance, rule, or statute related to claim or payment rights for persons in the signer's position that the signer has on the above referenced project to the following extent:

　　This release covers a progress payment for all labor, services, equipment, or materials furnished to the property or to _____ (person with whom signer contracted) as indicated in the attached statement(s) or progress payment request(s), except for unpaid retention, pending modifications and changes, or other items furnished.

　　The signer warrants that the signer has already paid or will use the funds received from this progress payment to promptly pay in full all of the signer's laborers, subcontractors, materialmen, and suppliers for all work, materials, equipment, or services provided for or to the above referenced project in regard to the attached statement(s) or progress payment request(s).

Signature: _____
Date: _____
Company Name: _____
By (w/ title): _____

STATE OF TEXAS　　§
COUNTY OF _____　§

　　This instrument was acknowledged before me on this _____ day of _____, 20____, by _____ (name), _____ (job title) of _____ (company name).

_____
NOTARY PUBLIC, STATE OF TEXAS

Kenneth Botwe

CONDITIONAL WAIVER AND RELEASE ON PROGRESS PAYMENT

Project _____

Job No. _____

On receipt by the signer of this document of a check from _____ (maker of check) in the sum of $_____ payable to _____ (payee or payees of check) and when the check has been properly endorsed and has been paid by the bank on which it is drawn, this document becomes effective to release any mechanic's lien right, any right arising from a payment bond that complies with a state or federal statute, any common law payment bond right, any claim for payment, and any rights under any similar ordinance, rule, or statute related to claim or payment rights for persons in the signer's position that the signer has on the property of _____ (owner) located at _____ (location) to the following extent: _____ (job description).

This release covers a progress payment for all labor, services, equipment, or materials furnished to the property or to _____ (person with whom signer contracted) as indicated in the attached statement(s) or progress payment request(s), except for unpaid retention, pending modifications and changes, or other items furnished.

Before any recipient of this document relies on this document, the recipient should verify evidence of payment to the signer.

The signer warrants that the signer has already paid or will use the funds received from this progress payment to promptly pay in full all of the signer's laborers, subcontractors, materialmen, and suppliers for all work, materials, equipment, or services provided for or to the above referenced project in regard to the attached statement(s) or progress payment request(s).

Signature: _____
Date: _____
Company Name: _____
By (w/ title): _____

STATE OF TEXAS §
COUNTY OF _____ §

This instrument was acknowledged before me on this _____ day of _____, 20____, by _____ (name), _____ (job title) of _____ (company name).

_____
NOTARY PUBLIC, STATE OF TEXAS

35

NOTICE:

This document waives rights unconditionally and states that you have been paid for giving up those rights. It is prohibited for a person to require you to sign this document if you have not been paid the payment amount set forth below. If you have not been paid, use a conditional release form.

<u>UNCONDITIONAL WAIVER AND RELEASE ON FINAL PAYMENT</u>

Project _____

Job No. _____

The signer of this document has been paid in full for all labor, services, equipment, or materials furnished to the property or to _____ (person with whom signer contracted) on the property of _____ (owner) located at _____ (location) to the following extent: _____ (job description). The signer therefore waives and releases any mechanic's lien right, any right arising from a payment bond that complies with a state or federal statute, any common law payment bond right, any claim for payment, and any rights under any similar ordinance, rule, or statute related to claim or payment rights for persons in the signer's position.

The signer warrants that the signer has already paid or will use the funds received from this final payment to promptly pay in full all of the signer's laborers, subcontractors, materialmen, and suppliers for all work, materials, equipment, or services provided for or to the above referenced project up to the date of this waiver and release.

Signature: _____

Date: _____

Company Name: _____

By (w/ title): _____

STATE OF TEXAS §

COUNTY OF _____ §

This instrument was acknowledged before me on this _____ day of _____, 20_____, by _____ (name), _____ (job title) of _____ (company name).

_____

NOTARY PUBLIC, STATE OF TEXAS

Form W-9
(Rev. October 2018)
Department of the Treasury
Internal Revenue Service

**Request for Taxpayer
Identification Number and Certification**

▶ Go to *www.irs.gov/FormW9* for instructions and the latest information.

Give Form to the requester. Do not send to the IRS.

1 Name (as shown on your income tax return). Name is required on this line; do not leave this line blank.

2 Business name/disregarded entity name, if different from above

3 Check appropriate box for federal tax classification of the person whose name is entered on line 1. Check only **one** of the following seven boxes.

☐ Individual/sole proprietor or single-member LLC ☐ C Corporation ☐ S Corporation ☐ Partnership ☐ Trust/estate

☐ Limited liability company. Enter the tax classification (C=C corporation, S=S corporation, P=Partnership) ▶

Note: Check the appropriate box in the line above for the tax classification of the single-member owner. Do not check LLC if the LLC is classified as a single-member LLC that is disregarded from the owner unless the owner of the LLC is another LLC that is not disregarded from the owner for U.S. federal tax purposes. Otherwise, a single-member LLC that is disregarded from the owner should check the appropriate box for the tax classification of its owner.

☐ Other (see instructions) ▶

4 Exemptions (codes apply only to certain entities, not individuals; see instructions on page 3):

Exempt payee code (if any)

Exemption from FATCA reporting code (if any)

(Applies to accounts maintained outside the U.S.)

5 Address (number, street, and apt. or suite no.) See instructions.

Requester's name and address (optional)

6 City, state, and ZIP code

7 List account number(s) here (optional)

Part I   Taxpayer Identification Number (TIN)

Enter your TIN in the appropriate box. The TIN provided must match the name given on line 1 to avoid backup withholding. For individuals, this is generally your social security number (SSN). However, for a resident alien, sole proprietor, or disregarded entity, see the instructions for Part I, later. For other entities, it is your employer identification number (EIN). If you do not have a number, see *How to get a TIN*, later.

Note: If the account is in more than one name, see the instructions for line 1. Also see *What Name and Number To Give the Requester* for guidelines on whose number to enter.

Social security number

☐☐☐ - ☐☐ - ☐☐☐☐

or

Employer identification number

☐☐ - ☐☐☐☐☐☐☐

Part II   Certification

Under penalties of perjury, I certify that:

1. The number shown on this form is my correct taxpayer identification number (or I am waiting for a number to be issued to me); and

2. I am not subject to backup withholding because: (a) I am exempt from backup withholding, or (b) I have not been notified by the Internal Revenue Service (IRS) that I am subject to backup withholding as a result of a failure to report all interest or dividends, or (c) the IRS has notified me that I am no longer subject to backup withholding; and

3. I am a U.S. citizen or other U.S. person (defined below); and

4. The FATCA code(s) entered on this form (if any) indicating that I am exempt from FATCA reporting is correct.

Certification instructions. You must cross out item 2 above if you have been notified by the IRS that you are currently subject to backup withholding because you have failed to report all interest and dividends on your tax return. For real estate transactions, item 2 does not apply. For mortgage interest paid, acquisition or abandonment of secured property, cancellation of debt, contributions to an individual retirement arrangement (IRA), and generally, payments other than interest and dividends, you are not required to sign the certification, but you must provide your correct TIN. See the instructions for Part II, later.

Sign Here

Signature of U.S. person ▶

Date ▶

General Instructions

Section references are to the Internal Revenue Code unless otherwise noted.

Future developments. For the latest information about developments related to Form W-9 and its instructions, such as legislation enacted after they were published, go to *www.irs.gov/FormW9*.

Purpose of Form

An individual or entity (Form W-9 requester) who is required to file an information return with the IRS must obtain your correct taxpayer identification number (TIN) which may be your social security number (SSN), individual taxpayer identification number (ITIN), adoption taxpayer identification number (ATIN), or employer identification number (EIN), to report on an information return the amount paid to you, or other

- Form 1099-DIV (dividends, including those from stocks or mutual funds)
- Form 1099-MISC (various types of income, prizes, awards, or gross proceeds)
- Form 1099-B (stock or mutual fund sales and certain other transactions by brokers)
- Form 1099-S (proceeds from real estate transactions)
- Form 1099-K (merchant card and third party network transactions)
- Form 1098 (home mortgage interest), 1098-E (student loan interest), 1098-T (tuition)
- Form 1099-C (canceled debt)
- Form 1099-A (acquisition or abandonment of secured property)

  Use Form W-9 only if you are a U.S. person (including a resident

Separate here and give Form W-4 to your employer. Keep the worksheet(s) for your records.

Form **W-4**	**Employee's Withholding Allowance Certificate**	OMB No. 1545-0074
Department of the Treasury Internal Revenue Service	▶ Whether you're entitled to claim a certain number of allowances or exemption from withholding is subject to review by the IRS. Your employer may be required to send a copy of this form to the IRS.	2019

1 Your first name and middle initial	Last name	2 Your social security number

Home address (number and street or rural route)

3 ☐ Single ☐ Married ☐ Married, but withhold at higher Single rate.
Note: If married filing separately, check "Married, but withhold at higher Single rate."

City or town, state, and ZIP code

4 If your last name differs from that shown on your social security card, check here. You must call 800-772-1213 for a replacement card. ▶ ☐

5 Total number of allowances you're claiming (from the applicable worksheet on the following pages) **5**

6 Additional amount, if any, you want withheld from each paycheck . . . . **6 $**

7 I claim exemption from withholding for 2019, and I certify that I meet **both** of the following conditions for exemption.
• Last year I had a right to a refund of **all** federal income tax withheld because I had **no** tax liability, **and**
• This year I expect a refund of **all** federal income tax withheld because I expect to have **no** tax liability.
If you meet both conditions, write "Exempt" here . . . . ▶ **7**

Under penalties of perjury, I declare that I have examined this certificate and, to the best of my knowledge and belief, it is true, correct, and complete.

Employee's signature
(This form is not valid unless you sign it.) ▶   Date ▶

8 Employer's name and address (**Employer:** Complete boxes 8 and 10 if sending to IRS and complete boxes 8, 9, and 10 if sending to State Directory of New Hires.)	9 First date of employment	10 Employer identification number (EIN)

For Privacy Act and Paperwork Reduction Act Notice, see page 4.   Cat. No. 10220Q   Form **W-4** (2019)

Form W-4 (2019)   Page **2**

income includes all of your wages and other income, including income earned by a spouse if you are filing a joint return.

Line G. Other credits. You may be able to reduce the tax withheld from your paycheck if you expect to claim other tax credits, such as tax credits for education (see Pub. 970). If you do so, your paycheck will be larger, but the amount of any refund that you receive when you file your tax return will be smaller. Follow the instructions for Worksheet 1-6 in Pub. 505 if you want to reduce your withholding to

don't complete this worksheet, you might have too little tax withheld. If so, you will owe tax when you file your tax return and might be subject to a penalty.

Figure the total number of allowances you're entitled to claim and any additional amount of tax to withhold on all jobs using worksheets from only one Form W-4. Claim all allowances on the W-4 that you or your spouse file for the highest paying job in your family and claim zero allowances on Forms W-4 filed for all other jobs. For example, if you earn $60,000 per year and

and 10 to comply with the new hire reporting requirement for a newly hired employee. A newly hired employee is an employee who hasn't previously been employed by the employer, or who was previously employed by the employer but has been separated from such prior employment for at least 60 consecutive days. Employers should contact the appropriate State Directory of New Hires to find out how to submit a copy of the completed Form W-4. For information and links to each designated State Directory of New Hires (including for U.S. territories), see

Form **941 for 2019:** **Employer's QUARTERLY Federal Tax Return**
(Rev. January 2019)   Department of the Treasury — Internal Revenue Service

950117

OMB No. 1545-0029

Employer identification number (EIN) ☐☐ – ☐☐☐☐☐☐☐

Name *(not your trade name)*

Trade name *(if any)*

Address
Number   Street   Suite or room number

City   State   ZIP code

Foreign country name   Foreign province/county   Foreign postal code

Report for this Quarter of 2019
(Check one.)

☐ 1: January, February, March

☐ 2: April, May, June

☐ 3: July, August, September

☐ 4: October, November, December

Go to *www.irs.gov/Form941* for
instructions and the latest information.

Read the separate instructions before you complete Form 941. Type or print within the boxes.

Part 1: **Answer these questions for this quarter.**

1 Number of employees who received wages, tips, or other compensation for the pay period
   including: *Mar. 12* (Quarter 1), *June 12* (Quarter 2), *Sept. 12* (Quarter 3), or *Dec. 12* (Quarter 4) **1** _____

2 Wages, tips, and other compensation . . . . **2** _____ . __

3 Federal income tax withheld from wages, tips, and other compensation . . . . . . **3** _____ . __

4 If no wages, tips, and other compensation are subject to social security or Medicare tax ☐ Check and go to line 6.

		Column 1		Column 2
5a	Taxable social security wages . .	_____ . __	× 0.124 =	_____ . __
5b	Taxable social security tips . . .	_____ . __	× 0.124 =	_____ . __
5c	Taxable Medicare wages & tips. .	_____ . __	× 0.029 =	_____ . __
5d	Taxable wages & tips subject to Additional Medicare Tax withholding	_____ . __	× 0.009 =	_____ . __

5e Add Column 2 from lines 5a, 5b, 5c, and 5d . . . . **5e** _____ . __

5f Section 3121(q) Notice and Demand—Tax due on unreported tips (see instructions) . . **5f** _____ . __

6 Total taxes before adjustments. Add lines 3, 5e, and 5f . . . . **6** _____ . __

9595 ☐ VOID ☐ CORRECTED

PAYER'S name, street address, city or town, state or province, country, ZIP or foreign postal code, and telephone no.	1 Rents $	OMB No. 1545-0115 2019 Form 1099-MISC	Miscellaneous Income
	2 Royalties $		
	3 Other income $	4 Federal income tax withheld $	Copy A For Internal Revenue Service Center
PAYER'S TIN	RECIPIENT'S TIN	5 Fishing boat proceeds $	6 Medical and health care payments $	File with Form 1096.
RECIPIENT'S name		7 Nonemployee compensation $	8 Substitute payments in lieu of dividends or interest $	For Privacy Act and Paperwork Reduction Act
Street address (including apt. no.)		9 Payer made direct sales of $5,000 or more of consumer products to a buyer (recipient) for resale ▶ ☐	10 Crop insurance proceeds $	Notice, see the 2019 General Instructions for
City or town, state or province, country, and ZIP or foreign postal code		11	12	Certain Information Returns.
Account number (see instructions)	FATCA filing requirement ☐	2nd TIN not. ☐	13 Excess golden parachute payments $	14 Gross proceeds paid to an attorney $	
15a Section 409A deferrals $	15b Section 409A income $	16 State tax withheld $	17 State/Payer's state no.	18 State income $

Form **1099-MISC**　　Cat. No. 14425J　　www.irs.gov/Form1099MISC　　Department of the Treasury - Internal Revenue Service

Do Not Cut or Separate Forms on This Page — Do Not Cut or Separate Forms on This Page

---

| Form **1120** Department of the Treasury Internal Revenue Service | **U.S. Corporation Income Tax Return** For calendar year 2018 or tax year beginning _____, 2018, ending _____, 20 ____ ▶ Go to www.irs.gov/Form1120 for instructions and the latest information. | OMB No. 1545-0123 **2018** |

A Check if:		B Employer identification number
1a Consolidated return (attach Form 851) ☐	TYPE OR PRINT	
b Life/nonlife consolidated return . ☐	Name	
2 Personal holding co. (attach Sch. PH) ☐	Number, street, and room or suite no. If a P.O. box, see instructions.	C Date incorporated
3 Personal service corp. (see instructions) ☐	City or town, state or province, country, and ZIP or foreign postal code	D Total assets (see instructions) $
4 Schedule M-3 attached ☐	E Check if: (1) ☐ Initial return (2) ☐ Final return (3) ☐ Name change (4) ☐ Address change	

Income	1a	Gross receipts or sales	1a	
	b	Returns and allowances	1b	
	c	Balance. Subtract line 1b from line 1a	1c	
	2	Cost of goods sold (attach Form 1125-A)	2	
	3	Gross profit. Subtract line 2 from line 1c	3	
	4	Dividends and inclusions (Schedule C, line 23, column (a))	4	
	5	Interest	5	
	6	Gross rents	6	
	7	Gross royalties	7	
	8	Capital gain net income (attach Schedule D (Form 1120))	8	
	9	Net gain or (loss) from Form 4797, Part II, line 17 (attach Form 4797)	9	
	10	Other income (see instructions—attach statement)	10	
	11	**Total income.** Add lines 3 through 10 ▶	11	
Deductions (See instructions for limitations on deductions.)	12	Compensation of officers (see instructions—attach Form 1125-E) ▶	12	
	13	Salaries and wages (less employment credits)	13	
	14	Repairs and maintenance	14	
	15	Bad debts	15	
	16	Rents	16	
	17	Taxes and licenses	17	
	18	Interest (see instructions)	18	
	19	Charitable contributions	19	
	20	Depreciation from Form 4562 not claimed on Form 1125-A or elsewhere on return (attach Form 4562)	20	
	21	Depletion	21	
	22	Advertising	22	
	23	Pension, profit-sharing, etc., plans	23	
	24	Employee benefit programs	24	
	25	Reserved for future use	25	
	26	Other deductions (attach statement)	26	
	27	**Total deductions.** Add lines 12 through 26 ▶	27	

05-158-A
(Rev.9-16/9)

Texas Franchise Tax Report - Page 1

■ Tcode

FILING REQUIREMENTS

Taxpayer number

■ Report year Due date

2018

Taxpayer name

Secretary of State file number
or Comptroller file number

Mailing address

| City | State | Country | ZIP code plus 4 | Blacken circle if the address has changed ■ ○ |

Blacken circle if this is a combined report ○ Blacken circle if Total Revenue is adjusted for Tiered Partnership Election, see instructions ○ Blacken circle to request a Certificate of Account Status ■ ○

** If not twelve months, see instructions for annualized revenue

Accounting year begin date** m m d d y y

Accounting year end date m m d d y y   SIC code   NAICS code

REVENUE (Whole dollars only)

				0	0
1. Gross receipts or sales	1. ■			0	0
2. Dividends	2. ■			0	0
3. Interest	3. ■			0	0
4. Rents (can be negative amount)	4. ■			0	0
5. Royalties	5. ■			0	0
6. Gains/losses (can be negative amount)	6. ■			0	0
7. Other income (can be negative amount)	7. ■			0	0
8. Total gross revenue (Add items 1 thru 7)	8. ■			0	0
9. Exclusions from gross revenue (see instructions)	9. ■			0	0
10. TOTAL REVENUE (item 8 minus item 9 if less than zero, enter 0)	10. ■			0	0

COST OF GOODS SOLD (Whole dollars only)

11. Cost of goods sold	11. ■			0	0
12. Indirect or administrative overhead costs (Limited to 4%)	12. ■			0	0
13. Other (see instructions)	13. ■			0	0
14. TOTAL COST OF GOODS SOLD (Add items 11 thru 13)	14. ■			0	0

COMPENSATION (Whole dollars only)

15. Wages and cash compensation	15. ■			0	0
16. Employee benefits	16. ■			0	0
17. Other (see instructions)	17. ■			0	0
18. TOTAL COMPENSATION (Add items 15 thru 17)	18. ■			0	0

PROCEED TO NEXT PAGE

State of _____   Rev. 1339F97

NOTICE TO TERMINATE LEASE FOR FAILURE TO PAY RENT

_____
_____
_____, _____, _____

To: Tenants Listed Above

You are hereby notified that you are indebted to me in the sum
of _____ for the rent and use of the premises located
at _____, _____, _____, _____, _____, now
occupied by you and that I demand payment of the rent or possession of the
premises within seven ____ days from the date of delivery of this notice, on or
before the ___ day of _____, 20___. Unless payment is made by such
date, the tenancy will be terminated.

This _____ day notice is provided to you based on your failure to pay rent and
pursuant to the applicable local and state statutes and regulations of the State.
You are further notified that legal action may be initiated against you unless you
pay the rent due or vacate the premises.

Signature: _____

Name of Landlord: _____
Address: _____
City, State, Zip: _____
Phone Number: _____

Date of Service: _____
Delivery Method: (Please check one)
        0 Hand Delivery   0 Registered Mail   0 Certified Mail   0 Posted

CHAPTER 5

WHOLESALING

Wholesaling is the act of getting a well below market value property under contract from a seller and assigning it to a buyer at below market value. It is still considered wholesaling if you buy a property well under market value and immediately resell at under market value. The person who finds the property places it under contract, and assigns them to a buyer is called a wholesaler. The one that buys at the wholesale price in order to use or resell may be a buyer, an investor, or both.

Regardless of the purpose, the property must have enough profit for both the wholesaler and the buyer for the wholesaling business to be sustainable. The person or institution that buys the property can use it or resell at retail price. To get the retail market value, they'll have to do any necessary repairs. Wholesaling requires very little money, and the risk is minimal, so it's a great entry into the world of real estate business.

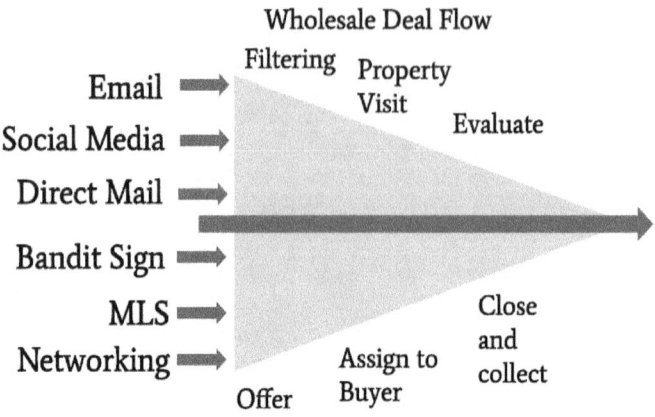

The seller who agrees to sell their property at well below market value is called a motivated seller. They are motivated to sell for a number of reasons. Most of the time, the chief reason among them is they're distressed. Since they need a solution, they tend to sell at a considerably lower price just to solve their problem. In such cases, they also can't afford to wait a long time before selling so they don't bother calling a realtor since going through that process can take longer than they desire.

As a wholesaler, you will be equipped with specialized knowledge to find these motivated sellers and offer to solve their problems. Your training will enable you to identify a motivated seller, get their property under contract, assign it to a buyer, and cash out at closing. Your skill will include knowing how to make an offer to both sellers and buyers, what documents to use, and how to keep a deal flow at all times. Your most precious commodity is your ability to bring sellers and buyers together and walk away with earnings for your involvement.

Imagine being able to start a real estate wholesaling business with little or no money and earn thousands of dollars per transaction. Then imagine doing a few transactions every month. That is precisely what I'm going to teach you.

Wholesaling is a process of finding properties well under market value, placing the property under contract, between you and the seller, and assigning the contract to a buyer at a higher price. You can do this with little or no risk since you're not the one buying the property.

You are merely the middleman or woman between the seller and the buyer. Here's how you do it. First, you locate a property owner who is distressed and motivated to sell. Then you get the owner to agree to sell at a specified price. We'll teach you how to evaluate the property and make an offer. Your contract will clearly stipulate that you are an investor and may find other investors to buy the property within a certain timeframe and at a profit.

Wholesaling Cycle

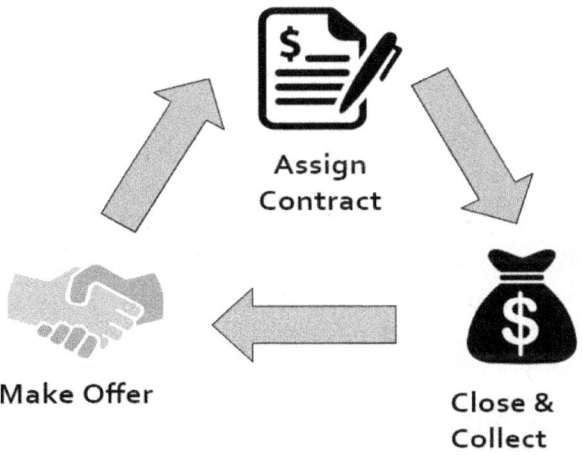

Assign Contract

Make Offer

Close & Collect

The key to maintaining your integrity and reputation is transparency. While locating properties that fit such wholesaling criteria, you're also locating investors that will buy at a marked-up price, but below market value. This way, that investor will also make a profit.

Upon finding the distressed seller, you place the property under contract with a document we call CONTRACT TO PURCHASE.

To show that you are serious, you pay a small deposit. Upon finding an investor who wants to buy the property, you secure an agreement with them through a document called AGREEMENT TO ASSIGN CONTRACT FOR SALE AND PURCHASE.

This document explains that you're not the owner of the property and you're only selling the contract. Although experience investors understand this concept, it is important to disclose this information for transparency. At this point, the buyer must pay a deposit to the title company to show that they are serious as well. In essence, your business is helping the motivated seller out of their situation, while saving investors time and money by looking for profitable deals.

EVERYONE WINS with this wholesaling business arrangement.

The seller is happy because you made it possible for them to sell their property faster than using a conventional method. The buyer is happy because they didn't have to find the seller on their own. At the time of closing, you will assign your contract to the buyer and COLLECT A NICE PAYCHECK. With this method of selling the contract, you get the full profit of your markup. In other words, if you get the property under contract for $250,000 and assign it for $275,000, then your profit is $25,000.

As I said, wholesaling is a business where you find houses that the owner is willing to sell well below market value. It also involves finding investors that are willing to buy houses at marked up prices, so long as you leave room for them to also make a profit. Lastly, this business also benefits from having lenders to fund the transactions. You don't need lenders for yourself, but it's good to refer them a new buyer if he or she doesn't have one. Notice I said business, meaning you have to make a profit.

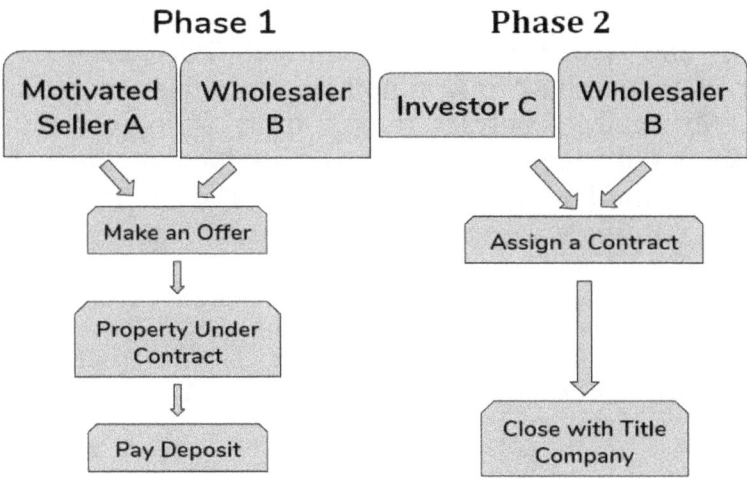

You may ask, why would anyone sell well below market prices? The answer varies, but in a nutshell, these people are doing what is best for them. They may be distress from a bad tenant, delinquent taxes, Pre-foreclosure, living in a different town than the property's location, in need of money, and many other unspecified reasons. No matter what their reasons are, these sellers are motivated to sell quickly and move on with their life.

Listing their property with a realtor the traditional way will take too long, so they need you to close the deal quickly and rescue them. I will explain in detail throughout the book as well as how to find these people and complete transaction after transaction as you grow your business. I'll also show you how to do wholesaling through banks and listing agents as well later in the book.

First, let's explore why wholesaling is an excellent choice as opposed to other forms of real estate business. For one, the time it takes to complete a transaction is very short. In as little as 30 days, you can complete multiple transactions and have cash in your hands or bank account. Once you do your first few deals, you'll gain experience and feel comfortable enough to do several deals simultaneously and on an ongoing basis.

Wholesaling is a great choice also because you can control any risk by the structure of your contract. For instance, your contract to purchase can stipulate a minimum deposit and time. My typical contract ranges from $500 to $1000 in deposit and about 10 hours of work from locating the house to closing on the house. The entire process is allotted 21 to 30 days to coordinate with all parties, including the seller, buyer, and Title Company.

These days, more old neighborhoods closer to town have properties that are being purchased by builders, torn down and rebuilt. Many of these marks the beginning of such projects immediately raises the value in that area. Often, there are a few vacant or abandoned houses in these areas. As a wholesaler, you can identify the owners of such properties and make an offer. In this scenario, the buyer is a builder who will tear down and rebuild. It's easy and fast because no one lives in these types of properties.

The wholesale model is not restricted to real estate only.

Nearly everything in business is purchased at wholesale and sold at retail, so real estate is no exception.

 Many individuals in the real estate business work in the capacity of broker or agents, developer or builder, legal or accounting, and other areas. Your focus can eventually broaden if you wish, but wholesaling is an excellent entrance into the world of real estate.

Make it a personal policy to be professional, courteous, and transparent. In fact, make sure you disclose to the seller that you'll make a profit after the deal is closed. Verify that they don't have a problem with it. I emphasize this point because although motivated sellers are informed that you will assign the property to another investor, they don't understand the time, effort, or specialized knowledge and its worth. They may feel your profit is too much and could get cold feet. Making a full disclosure about making a profit and getting their consent ahead of closing will prevent any second thought issues from arising. You don't want the seller to be surprised when you show up at closings to collect your check.

It is a business of carefully calculating the ending before you begin the process of putting a property under contract. By disclosing your intent to profit, you can determine through the seller's response if this will be a problem for him or her. In such cases, it's better to have a hard money lender so you can perform a double closing. Of course, this method costs a lot more; therefore, it changes your offer to the seller.

You'll factor in 2 closing cost and an inspection cost if you double close. The key is communication. The motivated seller needs a way out so if you can provide that in an upfront manner, the deal will succeed. Let them know that you can buy and resell, but your offer will be lower due to additional cost; however, if they are okay with you assigning to an investor, you can make a higher offer. In almost every case, your willingness to help the seller profit is welcomed when you make it clear in the beginning.

As for the buyer, they will not have any issues since you are assigning the contract to the property or selling at a wholesale price. Make it a principle to not waste your time or any party involved. You can accomplish this principle with transparency. After all, what sense does it make to pay a deposit, put a property under contract for 30 days only for it to fail in the end? Avoid overcomplicating things and be ready for a contingency such as buying and reselling if need be.

CHAPTER 6

FINDING MOTIVATED SELLERS

The business of wholesaling is a non-conventional way of doing real estate. This is because you are being trained to find deals well below market value. Since it's wholesale and not retail, you find deals through motivated sellers, put it under contract and assign it to investor buyers.

That buyer can then take further action such as live in it, remodel it, rent it, or sell it at retail or market value for profit.

Your job as a real estate wholesaler is to find properties well under market value.

We'll cover what a well under market value is in module 8 when we evaluate a property since each property is different.

A motivated seller is someone that wants to sell their property because it's not feasible for them to keep it. Their reasons vary most are a result of having multiple properties, unable to manage, inheritance, probate, divorce, foreclosure, absentee ownership, bad tenants, delinquent taxes, inability to upkeep, behind on payments, debt, bankruptcy, loss of job, etc.

These circumstances, over time, causes a potential seller to become motivated to solve this problem fast. You are the solution. You simply find them and make an offer to buy or find a buyer very quickly. Be upfront if you are strictly a wholesaler, but most wholesalers will eventually have the means to either buy or assign. An offer to buy or assign in 30 days is something that convention real estate agents can't do so you have the edge. Since the seller needs to solve their issue quickly, they are willing to sell for less than market value in exchange.

If a seller uses a real estate agent, it will take much longer, and they will pay a 6% commission. First, they'll have to clean the property. The agent will have to come or send someone to take some pictures. Seller will then have to fill out several forms and disclosures. When all that is completed, the agent will input this information in their database and list the property in the MLS. After that, assuming the house is appropriately priced, potential buyers will begin to make an appointment to come and walk through the house and ask many questions.

This could go on for some time before someone submits a letter of intent to buy. These letters of intent is not a contract to buy. It's only saying that they're interested. Buyer will then schedule an inspection which can be another week or two out. Once the inspector comes in and spends 3 to four hours in the property, they'll take a few more days to prepare an extensive report revealing every little thing that the seller didn't know was wrong with the property. The buyer may get scared off or may ask you to repair these things. Every potential buyer can put the seller through these steps. A seller may not have the money, time, or the desire to go through all of that.

As you can see, the conventional way is not feasible for a motivated seller that wants their problem solved quickly. This is why they are willing to drop the price and get rescued. The motivated sellers are out there, but they usually don't contact a real estate agent because they know how long it can take.

They also know they may have to spend money on repairs. Since they have no desire to prolong their situation, contacting them with an offer is like heaven sent.

Efforts Towards Direct Marketing

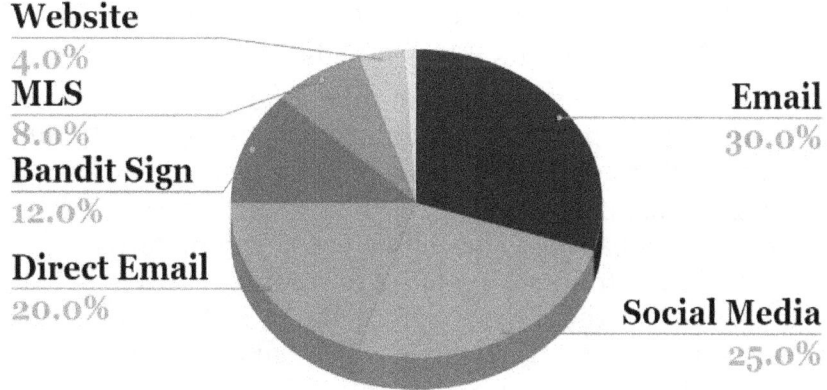

Website 4.0%
MLS 8.0%
Bandit Sign 12.0%
Direct Email 20.0%
Email 30.0%
Social Media 25.0%

There are many ways to locate and help motivated sellers for mutual benefit. You can begin by reaching out directly to them directly. Before contacting the seller, you must have your wholesale business set up with the following minimum:

1. Business Name and Logo
2. Business Cards and Brochure
3. Seller Know, Like & Trust Folder
4. Seller Intake Lead Form
5. Access to Internet
6. Contract to Purchase Form
7. Agreement to Assign Contract for Sale and Purchase Form

Start direct response marketing by reaching out to motivated sellers. This is my favorite method because it is unlimited, and it's a numbers game. The more people you reach out to, the more deals you make. You know their potential problem and know they need a solution. Craft a compelling message that speaks to their potential problem, then offer a solution. A way out for them would be to solve their property problem so they can get out of debt, save their credit, avoid probate, avoid bankruptcy, or just have money and be stress-free. You have to say all of this in the shortest way possible.

Billions of people socialize online with pictures, videos, stories, and comments. They spend a lot of time there. Reach out to motivated sellers on social media platforms such as Facebook, Instagram, Snapchat, LinkedIn, Pinterest, Twitter, etc. There are groups you can join that allow you to promote on certain days. The key is to join targeted groups and post consistently. Be sure to read their rules before posting. As you begin to make deals, you can buy ads on social media but be sure to test the conversion to make sure it's profitable.

You can also reach out to motivated sellers using direct mail. Simply send postcard consistently to a targeted group of sellers. The money you invest in marketing to a highly targeted list of motivated sellers will turn into huge profits. Sending postcards once or twice will not suffice. At a minimum, you should send to the same people at least 5 times over a period of 6 months. It's a numbers game and the more people you reach, the more deals you make.

Craigslist is a website of interconnected communities where people can buy and sell is the purpose of craigslist. Although this one is flooded with offers, it's relatively cheap and will give you exposure. Remember, you want to build a seller's list. Potential sellers choose not to sell now may sell later. Building a list that you can market to from time to time is part of an overall strategy you should adopt.

Craigslist is also an excellent website to cross-promote, network, and form partnerships and build teams. As you gain more experience, you'll fully understand the value of making these moves. The online tool is filled with sellers, buyers, investors, contractors, and the likes. The best part of it all is that they work in your local community.

Get people to notice you with a sign. There are so many people driving every day and strategically placing signs on routes where they work and play creates the awareness you need.

Before reaching out to potential sellers via yard signs or bandit signs, be sure to check with the local ordinance to make sure it's permissible. Not all areas allow this and violators may be fined, or signs may be removed.

Checking first ensures that you do the right thing, and your signs stay up longer. Unlike social media, direct mail and craigslist, the words/images on bandit signs have to be limited to no more than 5 for maximum effectiveness.

This is because people are driving and may not see or read everything. Make it simple so they can get the message and the telephone number.

Every potential seller that gives you their email and permission to email them can be added to your list. Building an email list is one of the most effective ways of marketing.

Once you start a list, it just continues to grow with your marketing efforts. Not everyone on your list will sell the first, second or even third time you contact them but some may eventually sell to you.

Build your list but don't spam them. Be considerate and only send them an offer periodically. When you begin to market your wholesale business actively, people will contact you.

Get their information and enter it into your database. At minimum, get their name, telephone number, email, and property address.

Emailing your list every 2 or 3 months is a good way to see if someone that didn't sell the first time is now ready to sell.

When you go out and establish relationships with like-minded people, you are networking. By getting out there and meeting other folks in real estate, you build a network of professionals that will send you referrals. It's free but time-consuming. The benefits are everlasting assuming you maintain a relationship with your contacts. Be helpful to others, and others will be helpful to you. This method can be very effective if you commit to attending networking events periodically.

Always have your sellers know, like & trust folder and a business card. Share these marketing tools and be sure to tell them what you do verbally. Make sure you have an objective or goal for each event and evaluate to see if you're meeting them at an acceptable and sustainable way. If you attend the right networking events and are of service to others, you'll get the same from them.

All professional realtors list properties for sale through the MLS. You may ask, why the MLS if realtors are the ones listing properties. Well, sometimes things don't go according to plan for the seller. If the seller fails to sell their property for too long, it loses its appeal, and suddenly no one wants it. This scenario may be a result of overpricing or some costly repair issue. Regardless, after so many Days on the Market or DOM, the seller may become motivated and sell at a significantly lower price.

A seller may also not want to deal with serious repair issues that were discovered during the inspection and may over-estimate the repair cost, thereby dropping the price well below market value. You can be a beneficiary of either circumstance that causes the seller to decrease price significantly. Since this method is time-consuming, contracting some folks to filter and present the properties that stand out in exchange for a commission if a deal made is practical.

CHAPTER 7

BUILDING A LIST

The integrity of real estate wholesaling business is dependent on building a list of sellers and buyers. You are the middleman, and nothing moves without the sellers and buyers. To build the list, you must employ the marketing methods, processes, and strategies we covered in section 5. As you begin to receive calls and emails, go ahead and build a list of sellers and buyers. You will surely do business with some of these people.

When you do, move them to a different list. For the rest, continue to market to them routinely via blasting texts and emails. Those that have not done business with you yet may do business with you in the future. As your list grows, you'll find some of the individuals replying to your email and text and inquire about future offers. Maintain a great relationship with the people on your list and keep them updated on any changes to your business.

It's essential that you build a know, like & trust credibility folder for sellers. Make it professional and clean. Keep your message simple and direct but specific. You want to create a seller's credibility folder that is catered to sellers. It should make them feel that you're here to ensure their burden is lifted. A seller must win in other for you to win. The folder should contain information that gives you credibility and therefore, easy to build trust.

In the event, you are unable to do business with the seller the first time, leave a credibility folder with them. This way, they can contact you at a future time. Make sure your seller folder includes pertinent information such as contact details and your main services. Include your picture, your business bio, and social proof such as testimonials.

It's also important that you create a know, like & trust credibility folder for buyers. It too should be professional and nice. Keep your message simple and direct but specific. Likewise, a buyer's credibility folder should be catered to buyers. It should be clear that you find wholesales properties and assign them below market values. A buyer must win if you want to win.

The folder should contain information that gives you

credibility and therefore, easy to build rapport. In the event, you meet an investor, or you are unable to complete a transaction with a buyer the first time, leave a credibility folder, and maintain a relationship. Most buyers are investors; therefore, they'll buy your future contracts. Make sure your buyer folder includes pertinent information such as contact details and your primary services. Include your picture, your business bio and social proof such as testimonials on this one as well.

Your marketing efforts are manifesting in calls and emails, and you are ready to answer and return calls. Remember that first impressions are a lasting one, so represent yourself and your business most professionally and courteously. Answer and make all calls by branding yourself from the very start. Say your name and your companies name and explain what services you offer.

For example, if I were promoting my educational company on an outgoing return call, I would say: Hi, this is Ken with Devise Wealth dot com, returning your call, how may I help you?

I would listen and write down their question; then I would say before I answer, let me tell you a bit about my background.

As an author of many financial literacy books, including **Little Money Big Credit** and my latest, **Pursuit of** ~~Happiness~~ **Assets**, it excites me when am able to be of service to actionable people. I also serve as director of education and publisher of many courses in building wealth with business, real estate, and investments to help people just like you. If you have a minute, I would like to ask a few questions to see how I can best answer your question.

When they consent, I would proceed to ask my questions and write notes on my student intake form. In essence, I've captured their need and ready to help them. I would then answer their questions. In this case, I would be able to guide the student to one of my courses or customize one on one coaching for them and tell them my availability. I would then ask them if they're ready to proceed.

If one on one is needed, we'll schedule it. I would confirm the date and time, extend thanks, and say goodbye for now.

Obviously, your approach would be different, but along those lines. In your case, you'll complete a seller lead intake form as the seller answers your questions. Your call will go like this: This is (Your name) with (Your company), returning your call. How may I help you? After listening to their desire to sell their property, you'll begin by confirming their full name. Proceed by telling them about your company and what you do. You can say something like this: *Our Company lifts the burden of mortgage, taxes, repair, and risk of bad credit off people. We can help you get out of unpleasant situation, and you don't have to pay 6% commission to a realtor. If you have a minute, I would like to ask a few questions so I can make you an offer. When they consent, go ahead and ask the questions on the form and write down their responses.*

Let's cover details of the form. The form has several sections. The first section is reserved for all the essential personal contact information and details about the property. Next, you want to know just how motivated the seller may be as well as details of the mortgage like balance, taxes, and liens, etc. This section is followed by asking price.

Don't make an offer right away, instead end by saying: we'll do an evaluation and call you back with an offer. Extend thanks and say goodbye.

The next step after lead intake is to perform a desktop evaluation. In addition to the completed seller lead intake form, run sales comparable via MLS or at least Trulia and Zillow if you don't have access to the MLS. On a side note, in most cases, developing a relationship with a realtor and agreeing to send your non-motivated sellers to them in exchange for access to the MLS is possible. Next, verifying ownership, address, property description, taxes, appraised value, and market value through tax appraisal office online can be done in most areas.

If everything checks out and sale price is below market value, you'll now visit the area of the property to see 3 or 4 comparable properties and the sale property itself to view landscaping, layout, exterior structures, interior, take pictures, and complete a repair estimate form. Call the seller and set an appointment for the property visit. Say: This is (Your name) again with (Your company), we are almost ready to make you an offer. We'll just need to do a site visit of your property, and then we can make the offer. Will 9 am on Saturday work for you? If not what day and time? Write down the date and time and say: We'll see you then, Thanks Bye

Call and confirm the appointment before heading out. Take notes of any unusual or remarkable things you see at the 3 or 4 comparable properties and the seller's property. When you arrive at the seller's property, knock on the front door, and introduce yourself. Have a clipboard in hand and repair estimate sheet. Write down everything you see that needs repair. Your folder should have seller lead intake, sales comparables, owner & tax info from the county and most important, an offer based on your calculations. Also, take a Contract Appointment Folder and have the papers inside as well as Contract to Purchase Form.

CHAPTER 8

MAKING AN OFFER AND PUTTING PROPERTY UNDER CONTRACT

Before you make an offer, be sure to add your asking price to the repair estimate. The total must be well below the market value to allow markup for your profit and buyer's profit. If the investors can't make a profit, they will not buy. You want a profit as well, so there must be room for both of you to make a profit and still solve the seller's problem. Make the offer in accordance with profit margins for you, the wholesaler, and the investor. It's okay if the seller's first price is not well below the market value because you will make your own offer after you complete your evaluations.

Here are your criteria for making an offer. First, you run a sales comparable. Then you determine the cost of repair to bring the property up to remolded standard or rehabilitation standard. Now you can make the offer. Always **offer wholesale price at well below the current competitive market rate, which is sales comps minus repair cost.**

The total of your offer should not exceed 75% under no circumstances if you're wholesaling. Typically 65% - 75% of market value.

It goes without saying that you should never ever offer 100% market value as a wholesaler even if the property is perfect. Let me demonstrate an example of a motivated seller with a house for sale. In the example given, if a house is worth $200,000 per sales comparable as covered in module 8, and you offer the maximum wholesale price with repair cost added at 75%, the dollar amount of your offer becomes $150,000.

If the repair cost is minor and estimated to be $5,000, then you have some room to make a profit and for the buyer to make a profit as well. In this case, if you sell the contract for $160,000, you make a $10,000 profit.

The investor that buys the property can expect to pay 3% in closing cost to the title company, which is $4,800 plus $5,000 in repairs leaving him or her a profit of $30,200. This is great for investors if they have plans for renting the property. However, if they turn around and sell, they can expect a 6% commission and another 3% closing cost of the after-market value or ARV for a profit of $12,200, which is still good.

As you can see, this deal is doable if the seller is willing to accept an offer of $150,000 for a $200,000 ARV of this property and the buyer has the down payment required to secure the loan short term. If the seller accepts your offer of $150,000 you can put this property under contract. This simply means you give the seller a deposit (usually $500) and the Contract to Purchase Form and you both sign to make it official.

After signing the contract with the seller, it is now time to contact the buyers and make your proposal. It wouldn't be hard to find a buyer to accept a contract assignment for $160,000 on a $200,000 property with $5,000 repair cost. You will assign this deal with ease and collect a check for $10,000 after closing it. It is much easier to build a list if you market to both buyers and sellers at the same time using your Buyers and Sellers know, like & trust folders. Just follow the strategies we covered in module 5.

Go ahead and contact your buyer's list and tell them about the property. They'll be ready to jump on the chance to make some cash and sign an Agreement to Assign Contract for Sale and Purchase. Maybe not so fast, because first the buyer must order an inspection to see what repairs need to be made and if there's a lender involved, they'll order an appraisal to see if the house is appraised at the market value. The two number usually differs but not by much. Make sure that you screen potential buyers to make sure they are capable of buying the property.

In other words, you should verify how they intend on paying for the property. If they are borrowing, ask for a pre-approval letter from the lender. If they are going to self-finance, ask for a financial statement. This process will protect you and prevent you from wasting time with buyers that can't buy. Remember that your contract with the seller is only 30 days so properly vet your buyers. In fact, you can prescreen the buyers before you do the deal since more deals will eventually come up.

After selecting a qualified buyer, proceed to sign the Agreement to Assign a Contract for Sale and Purchase. Buyer will follow up by ordering inspection and paying a deposit to the escrow or title company. Upon the result of the inspection by buyer and appraisal by the lender, a closing date can now be coordinated and scheduled. On that day all parties will show up at the designated office and once the documents are signed, you will receive your $10,000 check. That's it. You've completed your first wholesaling deal. Don't forget to pay your taxes.

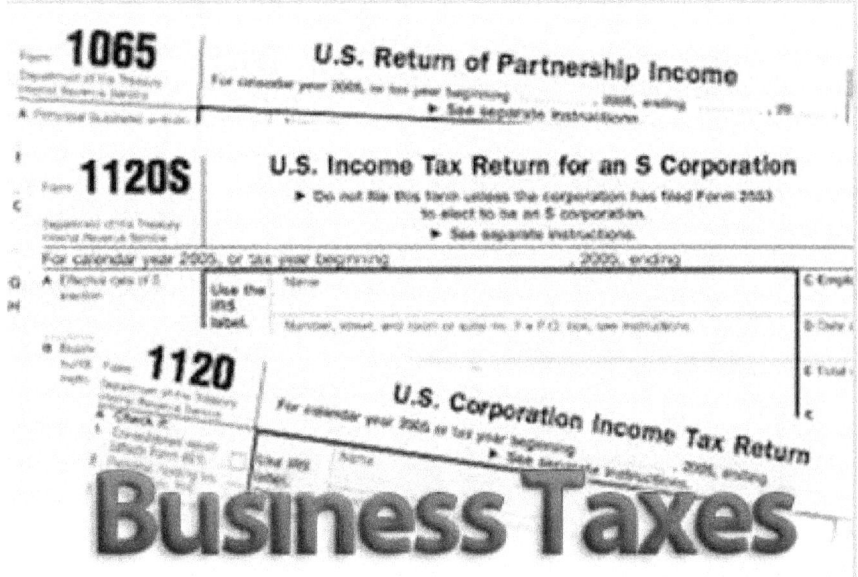

Filing taxes are part of running a real estate business. The extent of how much deduction breaks you receive is dependent on the experience and knowledge you have. More importantly, the tax accountant you choose can make a world of difference. I would not skip this step as a good accountant can save you a lot of money. They'll also know what documents to file to ensure compliance.

CHAPTER 9

FIX AND FLIP

In a fix and flip real estate business, you as an investor would start by formulating an entity by exploring my examples. You would then employ the strategies I teach to locate motivated sellers that are willing to sell well under market value. These initials are crucial as money in real estate rehab as it is sometimes called is made when you acquire the property. If you fail to buy properties at wholesale prices, you are fighting an uphill battle and may not make any profit after the repair. In the worst-case scenario, you could even take a loss. Take great measure to ensure your properties are purchased well under market value.

The next step is the construction and having the right contractors and holding them to a tights agreement is of utmost importance. There are a lot of contractors out there that will run circles around an untrained and experienced investor. They can make the rehab process a nightmare. Fortunately, I will give you everything you need to hold their feet to the fire, so the construction is completed on time and not overcharged. You also need to protect your assets at all time, and the renovation stages are no exception. I will tell you what documents to require of your chosen contractor at the beginning and the end of the project.

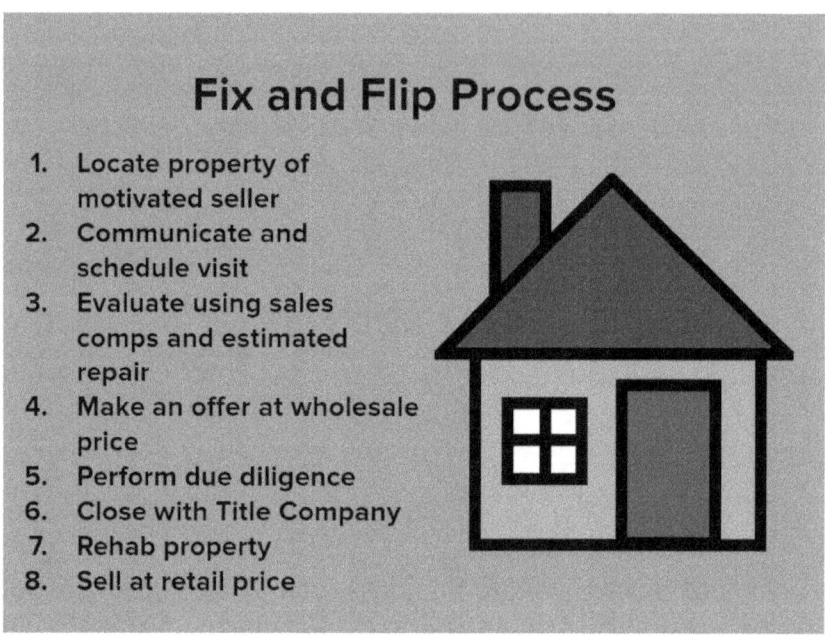

Fix and Flip Process

1. Locate property of motivated seller
2. Communicate and schedule visit
3. Evaluate using sales comps and estimated repair
4. Make an offer at wholesale price
5. Perform due diligence
6. Close with Title Company
7. Rehab property
8. Sell at retail price

Once the rehab is completed, you'll sell. This section will guide you on what to do before putting the property on the market. Your goal is to sell very quickly. To do it, the house must be properly presented and most importantly, correctly priced. We'll explore all of this, including how to close on the house with the title company. Everything that can be expected during closing will be discussed, and you'll finish reading this book, knowing exactly what to expect and what documents to take to closing. In its entirety, this section will take you through starting a fix and flip business and finding properties to selling it for huge profits.

Do you want to start a part-time business from home that will generate lots of money? What if I told you I have the right business for you that you can do without quitting your day job, for now?

This business requires no employees or inventory so you don't need much money to get started. Then I'll go on to you how you can even use other people's money or OPM to operate your business. Would you like that?

Of course, you would. Well, in the world of Real Estate Rehab or Flip and Fix as it is commonly called, you too can do this. First, you have to get the right training. You see the real estate that I'm talking about is far from the traditional one that 95% of individuals are doing.

It's not about going after what everybody else is after. The multiple listing service or MLS or even Foreclosure list at the auction is for the masses. I'm going to teach you about reaching out directly to the other 5% we call motivated sellers. These people find themselves in a situation and can use your help to get out of it. As a result, they are willing to sell their property well below market value. Think about it, if you had a house that was causing you serious ongoing distress, wouldn't you want relief?

Real Estate Fix and Flip business is about buying at wholesale prices, renovating the property and selling it at after repair value or retail price. The key to successfully doing this business and generating massive revenues is knowing the end before you begin. In other words, you must have an exit strategy. In a nutshell, you want the entire cost from start to finish to be less than the after-repair value or ARV. You also want to use other people's money or OPM to do the deal. The process will require locating a motivated seller and making an offer. Once the offer is accepted, you'll place the property under contract and do your due diligence.

Meanwhile the potential deal is presented to investors we call HARD MONEY LENDERS. If everything checks out, you'll close the deal using the hard money lender's money whom you can expect to pay an interest rate and maybe an origination fee and points. Your contractors are standing by to rehab the property so you can sell, pay everyone and take your profits.

With Fix and Flip, you can help a distressed seller out of their situation and make money for your lender. You can also pay the associated fees to contractors, Title Company, and maybe a realtor to list your finished property for quick sale at a fair retail price. You can do it all without using your own money.

When you buy a house or a property that needs repair at a discount and sell at market rate repairs, you have in fact just conducted a fix and flip. The real estate rehab business is nothing new, but many are approaching it wrong. Aside from looking for a deep discount, which is good, most people are searching in the same place. They tend to look to real estate agents and their MLS listings for deals. Although there are techniques that can be used to get good deals using the MLS, my first approach is always non- traditional.

I prefer to seek motivated sellers because the competition is very low. It also provides an opportunity to negotiate well. This is the case when there's no middleman or woman involved, such as an agent. Now, after the property is purchased, rehabbed and ready to be sold, I tend to reach out to agents to list the property but even then, I present the property to my own buyer's list as well.

At this point, it's first come first base, and with my buyers, I pay no commission.

There are so many things that must be learned by a relatively new fix and flip investor. It takes time, but some simple rules will always keep you on the right path. Among them are the previously mentioned. If you want the best possible deals, strictly look for off-market deals. Put the time in that's required and be an expert in due diligence. You must know how to uncover everything possible before you make a deal. Speaking of deals, learn how to structure it with creative financing whenever an opportunity presents itself. Motivated sellers are the best candidates for creative real estate.

You have to master the rehab process. Effective rehab managers get the best people for the best price. You want contractors that are fast and professional with little need for monitoring. After the renovation is completed, and the property is staged for showing, don't waste time with buyers that can't buy.

Make sure by requiring a pre-approval letter from a lender or financial statement. You can even go 1 step further by stipulating that they be pre-qualified by your own lender. This is the surest way to know if they'll get funded.

After evaluating the property, completing a repair estimate, making an offer, and signing the contract to purchase, you can now begin a walkthrough with the contractor of your choice. The purpose of this walkthrough is to stipulate what has to be completed throughout the entire property with your contractor. This checklist should be broken down by areas of the property, exactly what needs to be done, materials to be used, and estimated cost with product SKU. All of this should be captured in the scope of work, and this document will guide the contractor through the rehab process.

Scope of work is is a document that stipulates what is expected of general contractors and subcontractors. It is detail in nature and captures every little expectation for rehab of real estate. It helps minimize confusion among the parties. When you have a solid scope of work, contractors can bid on the job more accurately. At a minimum, a scope of work should include an overview of the project, deliverables, scope and schedule. The project manager should include payment details such as amount, intervals and how it is to be made. The breakdown in payments will also be included, so there's no confusion or delays.

During the walkthrough, take pictures as these will serve multiple purposes. It will be a reference point to contractors, buyers, and to others who it may concern. You'll take pictures again after completion of the rehab to serve the same mentioned purposes. It's good to place a lockbox with keys to the property so everyone involved could have access with ease and before leaving, place a yard sign promoting your business. The yard sign can be an image of your business card.

Fix and Flip is a business where investors find and buy houses well below market value, then rehab and sell at retail price for an attractive profit. The people who sell at well below prices are called motivated sellers. For one reason or another, they need to sell fast.

You, as the investor can use a number of resources to finance the purchase. You can use the seller through subject to or owner financing. You can fund the rehab through Fannie Mae Homestyle Renovation Mortgage, other rehab loans or from hard money lenders.

Before

After

You may ask, why would anyone sell well below market prices? The answer varies, but in a nutshell, these people are doing what is best for them. They may be distressed from a bad tenant, delinquent taxes, Pre-foreclosure, living in a different town than the property's location, in need of money, and many other unspecified reasons. No matter what their reasons are, these sellers are motivated to sell quickly and move on with their life. Listing their property with a realtor the traditional way will take too long, they need quick rescue. Fix and Flip business has huge profit potentials.

From purchasing and repairing all the way to selling, one complete transaction can be completed in as little as 90 days. Once you do your first few fix and flip, you'll gain experience and feel comfortable enough to do several deals simultaneously and on an ongoing basis.

You buy at wholesale and sell at retail. Rehabbing real estate can be an extremely profitable business for those that take the time to learn the right way. It involves being able to secure the property at well below market value, successfully rehabbing it per allotted budget as estimated and selling at after repair value or ARV.

Though it sounds relatively simple, there are a lot of bells and whistles that can't be overlooked. It's a project that must be managed both physically and with the contract agreement. First, you must understand your position as a real estate investor that rehab properties. You are basically taking over run-down houses and breathing life into them. The buyer is going to love it because of the restoration, and the neighbors will too. After all, a renovated property increases the neighborhood appeal and value of the properties nearby.

Your construction company of choice will do the work, and you'll manage them to make sure they fulfill the details of the contract with respect to permits, safety, price, time, and material. Your contractors will have general liability insurance and surety bond, so your assets are protected.

With each property that needs rehab, it is good to request 3 bids from general contractors. These contractors should be experienced with doing this type of rehab. The first thing you must do is verify and validate their business license.

Next, you should ask for three references from each bidder. Go ahead and check these references. As I mentioned before, this type of project takes a lot of money and time, so you don't want to be stuck with someone that is unprofessional, non-communicative, or simply incompetent. Doing your due diligence correctly will uncover any potential issues that could arise. If both the license and referrals check out, you may begin the negotiation. Negotiate for a turnkey solution.

That means the contractor you chose must handle everything from architectural drawings and work permits to inspections and certificate of occupancy or use-and-occupancy certificate if your municipality require them. You will be too busy to babysit any contractor. If you hire a general contractor, he will sub-contract some segments of the rehab, and it's fine but be sure that they are all paid and all sign a Waiver of Lien before you make the final payment.

During the negotiation, never disclose your budget. Allow them to submit bids based on material and labor and make sure the two are separate.

Materials used should be picked by you and be sure to verify cost and get copies of the receipt. Bring your scope of work during the bidding stage.

Make it clear to the contractors that you are looking at multiple bids, and they should give you their best competitive wholesale quote. All contractor quotes should be broken down per your scope of work. Do not hesitate to negotiate after you get all your bids before making a decision.

As you gain more experience, you can begin to subcontract if you can do it efficiently but for now, let them handle it all from start to finish.

The contractor must agree to your terms in writing. If you want something and it is not in writing, you most likely won't get it.

All the mentioned preparations should be done while the property is under contract so as soon as you close on the property, you can have the contractor sign your documents, pull permits, and start the job.

The Scope of Work and Independent Contractor Agreement Form should be signed before work begins, and have the contractor sign a 1099 form as well as a Final and Unconditional Waiver of Lien form upon completion of the rehab.

The Independent Contractor Agreement must cover every expectation, including documents that needs to be signed before final payment is made.

For instance, the General Contractor or GC should have General Liability Insurance with you added as additional insured before they begin the rehab.

Stipulate the payment intervals and be sure not to release more than fifty percent of the entire amount until completion of the job and your punch list has been addressed. It is assumed that a professional contractor has the capital to begin the job before demanding the first payment. Properly file your copy for future reference and business documentation. Break the rehab into three phases and release funds after the completion of each phase. This will save you time in streamlining the project.

The first phase is cleaning out and framing. During this phase, anything that needs to be replaced will be removed, and carpenters will redo any framing needed. The second phase is rough out, and it involves electrical wiring, HVAC, plumbing, and roof work. After the rough out inspection is completed, the third phase will begin. This includes insulation and then finishing sheetrock, trimmings, paint, and flooring.

After all final inspections are signed off, a certificate of occupancy will be issued if it's required in your municipality. Put contingency clause in place to make sure contractors stick to the timeline and pass all inspections. Put another one that penalizes the contractor if the job is not finished at least 1 week after the proposed completion date.

For instance, you could include in the agreement that the contractor will pay you a certain amount per day if he fails to complete the job one week after the due date. Explain to the contractor that any deviation from the scope of work will be a problem but fulfilling it means repeat business for them.

When you run your business like a business, they will know you mean business and do all they can to meet the stipulated deadlines. It is therefore important to meet with the contractor and all his sub-contractors on the job site before work begins to go over everything one more time.

They will not neglect your rehab for other jobs. Do perform a walk-through with the contractor after each phase of the job is completed, including the last. Remember the inspectors are there to inspect code and safety aspects of the rehab. Your job is to check to see if all the specifications, add-ons, improvements, and cosmetics are completed per agreement. Do not release the final payment until everything is completely done per the Independent Contractor Agreement and Scope of Work.

Check the walls, ceilings, floor, plumbing, electrical, paint, A/C, water heater, kitchen, bathrooms, roof, landscaping and any other item that was to be completed using a punch list. Write the final check when everything is properly completed. Be sure to get the W9 Tax Form and the Final, and Unconditional Waiver of Lien signed before releasing the final check. The rehab is now complete, and you are ready to sell and move on to the next one.

Schedule a few more essential steps to make sure the house sells fast. Dispatch your house cleaning crew to thoroughly clean the house inside and out including mowing the yard and trimming trees etc.

Invest by having the house professionally staged with furnishings and have professional photos of both inside and outside taken.

You want the house staged because it is proven that houses that are staged sells faster than those that are not.

The photos will serve multiple purposes, such as documentation and marketing.

Once all these essential steps have been taken, change the lockbox code, and you are now ready to show the house at fair market retail price.

Have your assistant show the house to your own buyer's list while your realtor shows the house to buyers from the MLS. Again, it is important for you to price the house correctly the first time. With a newly renovated house and the correct market value pricing, your house could sell in the first week. It is better to price it right and sell quickly than to reduce the price later if it fails to sell. Remember, the more days on the market or DOM, the less appealing it appears to buyers.

With each property that needs rehab, it is good to request 3 bids from general contractors. These contractors should be experienced with doing this type of rehab. The first thing you must do is verify and validate their business license.

Next, you should ask for three referrals from each bidder.

Go ahead and check these referrals. As I mentioned before, this type of project takes a lot of money and time so you do not want to be stuck with someone that is unprofessional, non-communicative or simply incompetent.

Doing your due diligence correctly will uncover any potential issues that could arise. If both the license and referrals check out, you may begin the negotiation. Negotiate for a turnkey solution. That means the contractor you chose must handle everything from architectural drawings and work permits to inspections and certificate of occupancy or use-and-occupancy certificate if your municipality require them. You will be too busy to babysit any contractor.

If you hire a general contractor, he will sub-contract some segments of the rehab and it's fine but be sure that they are all paid and all sign a Waiver of Lien before you make the final payment.

During the negotiation, never disclose your budget. Let them submit bids based on material and labor and make sure the two are separate. It should be the material you picked and be sure to verify material cost and get copies of the receipt.

Bring your scope of work during the bidding stage. Make it clear to the contractors that you are looking at multiple bids and they should give you their best competitive wholesale quote. All contractor quotes should be broken down per your scope of work. Do not hesitate to negotiate after you get all your bids before making a decision. As you gain more experience, you can begin to subcontract if you can do it efficiently but for now, let them handle it all from start to finish.

Rehabbing real estate can be extremely profitable business for those that take the time to learn the correct way. It involves being able to secure the property at well below market value, successfully rehabbing it per allotted budget as estimated and selling at after repair value or ARV. Though it sounds fairly simple, there are a lot of bells and whistles that cannot be overlooked. It's a project that must be managed both physically and with contract agreement.

First you must understand your position as a real estate investor that rehab properties. You are basically taking over run-down houses and breathing life into it. The buyer is going to love it because of the restoration and the neighbors will too. After all, a renovated property increases the neighborhood appeal and value of the properties nearby. Your construction company of choice will do the work and you'll manage them to make sure they fulfil the details of the contract with respect to permits, safety, price, time, and material. Your contractors will have general liability insurance and surety bond so your assets are protected.

The contractor must agree to your terms in writing. If you want something and it is not in writing, you most likely won't get it. All the mentioned preparations should be done while the property is under contract so as soon as you close on the property, you can have contractor sign your documents, pull permits and start the job. The Scope of Work and Independent Contractor Agreement Form should be signed before work is started and have contractor sign a 1099 form as well as a Final and Unconditional Waiver of Lien form upon completion of the rehab. You can download a copy of these forms to use as reference.

The Independent Contractor Agreement will cover every expectation, including documents that needs to be signed before final payment is made. For instance, the General Contractor or GC should have General Liability Insurance with you added as additional insured before they begin the rehab. Stipulate the payment intervals and be sure not to release more than fifty percent of the entire amount until your punch list after the completion of the job has been addressed. It is assumed that a professional contractor has the capital to begin the job before demanding the first payment. Properly file your copy for future reference and business documentation.

Break the rehab into three phases and release funds after the completion of each phase. This will save you time in streamlining the project. The first phase is cleaning out and framing. During this phase, anything that needs to be replaced will be removed and carpenters will redo any framing needed. The second phase is rough out and it involves electrical wiring, HVAC, plumbing, and roof work. After the rough out inspection is completed, the third phase will begin. This includes insulation and then finishing sheetrock, trimmings, paint, and flooring. After all final inspections are signed off, a certificate of occupancy will be issued if it's required in your municipality.

Put contingency clause in place to make sure contractors stick to the timeline and pass all inspections. Put another one that penalizes the contractor if the job is not finished at least 1 week after the proposed completion date. For instance, you could include in the agreement that the contractor will pay you a certain amount per day if he fails to complete the job one week after the due date. Explain to contractor that any deviation from the scope of work will be a problem but fulfilling it means repeat business for them.

When you run your business like a business, they will know you mean business and do all they can to meet the stipulated deadlines. It is therefore important to meet with contractor and all his sub-contractors on the jobsite before work begins to go over everything one more time.

 They will not neglect your rehab for other jobs. Do perform a walk-through with the contractor after each phase of the job is completed including the last. Remember the inspectors are there to inspect code and safety aspects of the rehab. Your job is to check to see if all the specifications, add-ons, improvements, and cosmetics are completed per agreement.

COMPLETED CHECKLIST

Do not release the final payment until everything is completely done per the Independent Contractor Agreement and Scope of Work. Check the walls, ceilings, floor, plumbing, electrical, paint, A/C, water heater, kitchen, bathrooms, roof, landscaping and any other item that was to be completed using a punch list. Write the final check when everything is properly completed. Be sure to get the W9 Tax Form and the Final and Unconditional Waiver of Lien signed before releasing the final check.

The rehab is now complete and you are ready to sell and move on to the next one. Schedule a few more essential steps to make sure the house sells fast. Dispatch your house cleaning crew to thoroughly clean the house inside and out including mowing the yard and trimming tress etc. Make the investment by having the house professionally staged with furnishings and have professional photos of both inside and outside taken.

You want the house staged because it is proven that houses that are staged sells faster than those that are not. The photos will serve multiple purposes such as documentation and marketing.

Once all these essential steps have been taken, change the lockbox code and you are now ready to show the house at fair market retail price. Have your assistant show the house to your own buyers and your realtor show the house to buyers from the MLS. Again, it is important for you to price the house correctly the first time. With a newly renovated house and the correct market value pricing, your house could sell in the first week. It is better price it right and sell quickly than to reduce price later if it fails to sell. Remember, the more days on the market or DOM, the less appealing it appears to buyers.

CHAPTER 10

EXIT STRATEGY

If you've taken any of my real estate courses, you know that I'm very big on exit strategy. That is when you start with an end in mind. By doing so, you've already answered questions such as how do I plan to profit from the investment, and if that fails, what is my second option? It is important to plan an exit strategy in real estate as a business. In the case of fix and flip, the main question has already been answered, but what is plan B and how is it executed?

Determine your ideal market and how to get your newly renovated house in front of potential buyers in the very best presentation possible. Figure out how long it should take to flip and cash out. Careful planning ensures that you have the entire process under control. To be safe, factor in an additional 15% percent in renovation cost and 10% less in sale price. If you calculate a profit after these contingency factors are added, you should be fine.

Fix and flip is a business that a conventional lender doesn't like to fund because of its short term nature. As a result, many investors turn to hard money lenders. Hard money lenders are private investors that let their money work for them by lending to buyers when convention lenders won't. Cases of having multiple loans or the need for renovation loans makes it very hard to secure from a regular lender.

Hard money lenders typically do a 70% Loan to Value or LTV of the "As IS" value. They limit their investment to this amount to make sure the buyer has "skin in the game." Keep in mind that these people or institutions are investors too and some charge within the range of 10% to 15% interest only plus some charge an origination fee of 3% to 5%.

Some hard money lenders also charge points, which equals 1% of the loan amount. For example, if you're charged 5 points on $100,000, then you will pay $5000. In real estate business, you win when you buy, so finding motivated sellers that are willing to sell at 70% below after repair market value with a repair and closing cost is a deal.

That means a $200,000 after repair value property for $140,000 will produce $60,000 minus the hard money lender's interest, real estate, and closing fees.

Even at 15% interest ($3500) plus 5% origination fee ($7000) from hard money lender, you'll see make $31,500 profit if it takes 6 months from the purchase date to date of sale, and that's including 9% ($18,000) in real estate and closing fees.

Knowing your numbers puts you in a position to have a clear and precise exit strategy so that you don't spin your wheels in the process of making a transaction. You must know the after-repair value for that immediate area, and every single significant cost that will be associated with the property from deposit all the way to closing the sale after all rehab is completed.

Any expense that is missed could mean a higher offer than what should have been made. Missing enough details in cost can put you at a loss when the property is finally sold. It doesn't make sense to invest time and money into any business and not gain an attractive ROI. Even non-profit organizations have return on investment so adopt the attitude of not losing in any business deals.

I lost on several deals in the beginning because I lacked the experience of dealing with contractors. Since then, I have developed a solid process through contract that will put any contractor feet to the fire. Imagine a contractor not showing up to the job every day and subcontractors coming in drunk and sleeping on the job. Then imagine the same contractor asking to be paid every few days yet you don't see any progress. Confrontations of these issues only made matters worse since the contractor has managed to collect most of the money not proportional to the work completed.

When you finally get fed up and ask the contractor to leave, you are left with little or no money to hire another contractor to finish the job. Even worse, the previous contractor somehow has his attorney attempt to collect the remainder of the money. I've seen it all and navigated my way through it. In the end, I have become very savvy in handling contractors. Such experiences are not only limited to dealing with general contractors because I could tell you lots of incidents where outcomes were equally unpredictable.

The point that I'm conveying here is that you should plan for the best but be ready to adapt if anything less than the best occurs. I want you to start every real estate transaction with an exit strategy so that when something goes wrong, you can limit losses and move on. It is better to minimize a loss, learn from it, and move on to fine-tune your systems than to drag on something indefinitely and deplete your resources in the process.

A good exit strategy allows you not to lose or at least minimize your losses during a regular transaction or when the unforeseen happens. Every serious business owner has a few of these in their back pocket and will not hesitate to utilize it when warranted. You should do the same.

CHAPTER 11

CREATIVE FINANCING

Buying real estate without a bank loan or down payment is what creative financing is all about. Even when you are capable of securing loans, learning to use other people's money or resources will enable you to do more and more deals without reaching a cap. Creative financing is only limited to your imagination. There are many ways to structure this type of deals. The basis for an owner agreeing to creative financing is usually a result of lack of desire or not being able to pay the mortgage. When you find these owners, taking a creative approach that will relieve them of the monthly payments is usually all they want. Just make sure that any loans you take over are fixed and not variable.

The first one is called owner financing. With this scenario, you'll negotiate with an owner who has no mortgage to finance the deal for you. Usually, these types of owners either inherited or pay it off over the years and have no interest in being a landlord. You can rent the property after purchase and use some of the proceeds to pay the landlord.

Knowing what type of questions to ask in order to uncover the seller's motivation is extremely important in structuring creative financing. It allows you to see their situation, and therefore, you can construct a deal that will benefit you both. For example, an owner that has a 100% paid off property but lives out of town may be willing to do an owner financing deal. They want to sell the property, and you want to acquire it with little or no money.

Owner financing has many benefits, including the avoidance of some closing cost that is charged when lenders are involved. These fees can be up to 3% of the purchase price.

Doing a deal like this also means you can ask for a zero interest or at least negotiate a lower interest rate than what lenders are currently charging.

With the right motivation, the seller will meet your terms and price so long as you are masterful in negotiating what you want. Regardless of your level of skills, you should make deals that are mutually beneficial to both parties. It's just good business, and it helps keep your reputation intact. A good name is worth more than any amount of wealth is a philosophy I adopted since the days of my youth.

The second type of creative financing involves taking over the existing financing of a property. It is called subject to, where the owner transfers the deed to the buyer but not the mortgage. A small segment of homeowners who wants out are willing to do the deal this way. Buyer takes over the mortgage payments and avoids all the requirements of getting a loan and making down payment and closing cost. This is possible because the bank just wants the monthly payments and don't care who makes the payments.

Before doing a subject to, be sure to do a title search to make sure there aren't any liens on the property.

You may ask, why would any seller do a subject to? Well, let's say that a seller is facing pre-foreclosure. They lost their high paying job to artificial intelligence, and the prospect of finding another job is not good. At the same time, the seller has a mortgage he or she can't afford to pay. They are in the process of losing their home and getting bad credit. This type of motivated seller may be willing to stop the bleeding by accepting an offer such as a subject to. They know that if mortgage payments become current consequent ones are paid on time, they will possibly save some equity and their credit. These factors can be used to strategize a deal that benefits both the seller and the buyer.

Then there's a lease option where you don't own but just lease with the option to buy in the future. With this option, the owner stays on the deed of trust and mortgage, but you have an option to buy after a certain amount of years.

Owners that do this type of deal are usually relocating to another place and having problem selling outright. They may also be in need of money in the form of a down payment as part of the option. There are many more reasons why sellers may accept a lease option deal. You, as an investor, must know why you want that option. Some of the more prominent reasons are equity and cash flow.

The key to creative financing is to identify what chief distress the seller is having and tailor a solution to their problem. For this reason among others, it is good to use the seller lead intake form, which will help anyone to ask the important questions so that a solution can be proposed. The more you are involved in creative financing, the better you become.

You can do creative financing for renters/buyers as well. There's much to be gained with rent to own strategies. Imagine being able to secure a large down payment we call option as part of the agreement. Down payment can easily be $10,000 or more for a rent to own deal and it is non-refundable. This money could be used as another down payment for your next property.

Put a rent to own sign out near the property and watch how many calls come in. Have a dedicated line with voicemail for this because the calls can become overwhelming.

You'll need to have your attorney draft a rental agreement as well as an option agreement. The rental agreement will stipulate the terms such as rent amount, deposit, and who pays for repairs. Since it's a rent to own, you'll make the renter responsible for repair and maintenance. This will save you huge amount of money in maintenance cost. You can then turn around and use these savings to structure rent credits in your option agreement and benefit yet again by raising the rent a bit more than the standard prices for traditional renters.

In other words, instead of giving rent credit for, let's say $100 a month out of the monthly payment to go towards equity for the option buyer, you give $200. A two-year rent to own will accumulate almost $5000 in equity, so rent to own customers love it.

They also appreciate the time because it gives them the ability to clean up their credit and save money or just prepare to become a home buyer. Just be sure to offer rent credit as a result of on-time monthly payments.

When the rent to own term ends, the buyer will then go out and secure a loan to purchase your property at the agreed price on the option agreement. This price is usually the appraised value of the property. Be sure to check your local laws concerning rent to own and lease option. If the term ends and the rent to own customer does not buy, you can do another deal with them or part ways. Screening and selecting your tenants wisely by using the criteria I've outlined in chapter 13 will help you prevent problems. Remember the "skin in the game" strategy, the higher the down payment you require from your rent to own tenant, the more success you'll have.

CHAPTER 12

CLOSING AND GETTING PAID

I've emphasized throughout this book the need to be transparent. Besides it being the right thing to do, not being upfront can cause issues during closing. In the case of wholesaling, let's say you didn't disclose to the seller that you'll be assigning the contract for a profit and they discovered this fact at the time of closing. The seller could easily refuse to sell and let you walk away with a hefty profit. They may feel like you don't deserve and may not really understand your position in the process. Be honest and forthcoming from the very start by telling the seller your intent to assign the contract and by telling the buyer that you are acting as a wholesaler.

Most issues arise during closing when there's lack of transparency, but it can also happen when the profit margin for the wholesaler is substantial as in over $10,000. In such cases, it may be easier to double close. Beware, double closing comes with additional cost. You'll pay closing cost twice and down payment if lending is required as well as an appraisal fee.

It is a safe way to transact when you have a large profit margin and want to avoid the risk of the seller getting cold feet because of your involvement as a wholesaler. It is not fair to spend money and time to find a motivated seller and get a property under contract only to have the deal collapse. For this reason, be prepared to do double closing if there's substantial profit to be gained.

Again, if the deal closes with you as a wholesaler, you'll walk away with all your profit without having any down payments or fees. You don't even have to pay for an inspection unless you want one during your evaluation stage. Your biggest effort is matching a seller with a buyer and taking a profit through your mark-up.

However, if you know the seller's price is considerably well below market value after your evaluation and you have access to the funds, go ahead and double close. This strategy will prevent any unforeseen issues that may arise as a result of you transferring contract. In in the instance of double closing, additional expenses are incurred but using this training; you can anticipate all cost by doing your calculations before and after your offer is accepted.

As the name implies, double closing means you'll have to close two times. You'll close by buying the property and close again by selling it to an investor. It is not an efficient way to conduct wholesaling, but if seller either refuse to sign the contract to purchase or just non-cooperative on the deal, your best bet is to take this route especially if there's profit in the deal.

Double closing is not only limited to a wholesaler. A real estate investor that does fix and flip may also double close but usually the time frame from the first to the second closing is extended by weeks or months. Certain closing fees associated with closing twice, however, cannot be avoided. What can be avoided are commissions when you buy since the seller is responsible for paying it. You will also not have to pay the lender's closing fees when you sell because it is reserved for the buyer.

One fee that is well worthwhile selling after the rehab is the broker/agent commission. Think about it; you've gone through the process of finding a property under value and rehabbing it using your contractor and are now ready to sell. You don't make any money until you sell; therefore, selling quickly should be your primary aim. You can sell quickly by having an agent list your property in the MLS. You can even negotiate a lower commission than the standard 6% but not using the MLS at all in the name of saving could be regrettable.

This is why it is so important to calculate all the associated closing fees and rehab expenses as well as the ARV of the property before making an offer. Not taking the process seriously could be the difference between success and failure in real estate business, especially fix and flip where you are going to close a total of two times at some point. Use all the tools that have been provided to properly evaluate the property and make a sensible and profitable offer. If you cannot make a profit comfortably on a deal, turn it down.

Closing for rental income property as much easier because you're only buying. Even when you complete the rehab and do a cash-out refinance, you'll pay less than if you were to sell. The point is to know the type of deal you are doing so you can apply the correct strategy. The end result for any of the investments you choose is to make a profit.

Whether it's wholesaling, fix and flip or rental income properties, you are doing it for a profit, therefore, visualize the end before the beginning. Close and cash out from assigning a contract if you are a wholesaler, close and get a check for fix and flip if you rehab and sell houses or simply do a cash-out refinance and pull out your equity with rental income properties. In other words, don't engage in any transaction if you cannot close and get paid.

CHAPTER 13

RENTAL INCOME PROPERTIES

In the world of real estate rental income properties, many wonderful benefits are available for those that recognize them through proper training. In this section, I will show you everything you need to quickly set up your rental house business and start enjoying these benefits. We'll cover how to properly structure a real estate rental business and the other forms of asset protection. The lessons you learn will help you with setting up your business correctly with maximum benefits.

We'll then dive into finding properties well below market value. Doing it this way allows you to start off with some equity, and you'll learn strategies to strip the equity for the next property you acquire. Then we'll get into the real reason for rental property, cash flow. I'll walk you through the fundamental of what to buy, how to rehab, and things that should be covered and sign with the contractor to keep them honest.

This step can make or break your business, so we'll spend time dissecting scope of work and upon completion of the rehab, we'll go into how to position the property for fast rental and profitable rental. Everything you need to know from properly screening tenants to renting for passive income will be covered.

Rental income property has many benefits. When done properly, an investor can build wealth through a host of means. The first of the benefits is cash out refinance. In this scenario, a strategic investor would purchase a property that costs plus repairs are well under market value. This buyer will start by identifying such properties through direct response marketing.

It entails reaching out to people who for one reason or another, are motivated to sell. Often, these people must sell now! We will cover various reasons that cause sellers to be distressed throughout the section. In this example of cash out refinance, the investor will have some equity when the deal is closed, and rehab has been completed. The investor will then ask a mortgage lender to refinance the maximum loan-to-value of the after-repair value of the property.

Banks and other lenders usually allow an 80% loan-to-value. For instance, an ARV of a $200K house would have an LTV of $160K.

Let's say the investor spent his or her own money to acquire the property and do the rehab; they will get a check for $160K. The difference between the total cost of the property/repair and the LTV of $160K is your cash out. Of course, you can expect closing fees of about 3%.

This money can be used to do another deal, then another, and so forth. Perfecting this strategy will not only generate cash but also increase your net worth. Congratulations, you have begun building wealth. The next means of building wealth through rental income properties is cash flow. This concept is elementary because the difference between your monthly rent minus your expenses such as mortgage payment, homeowner's insurance, maintenance, etc. should be positive. The more your cash flow, the better, but all the numbers have to be factored in at the time of purchase.

The benefits don't end here because the landlord also enjoys a nice tax break called depreciation, and it is allowed for twenty-seven and a half years from the time you purchase a property. Meanwhile, the rental property is growing in equity year after year through appreciation as well as mortgage pay down. It is important to perform rentals as a wealth building tool, especially for new investors.

From the richest man and woman in the world to the working class, everyone needs passive income. What is passive income, you might ask? First, let me tell you what it is not. It is not earned income like a typical 9 to 5. Neither portfolio nor active, passive income is cash flow you get on a regular basis with little or no effort to maintain it. My friends, the best candidates for passive income is real estate rental properties.

For one, you'll have monthly cash flow from your properties. Secondly, you'll get 27 ½ years of money in tax breaks that accountants call depreciation. Third, you'll build equity, meaning an increase in value over time. What you paid for the property today is worth more tomorrow.

Shall I go on? Okay, as you pay down the principal, the equity grows even bigger; therefore, you can strip the equity in a couple of years and buy another real estate rental property.

Do you see where I'm going with this? Follow me like social media, because it gets more beautiful. You can buy these rental properties with other people's money. Yes, Lenders and other investors will give you the money you need to get the passive income you want through buy and hold. How sweet is that? Now, before you get started, I have to tell you that it's not as simple as it sounds, but it's easy. I'll show you how to get a zero-down payment for your first deal.

I'll also show you how to find properties well below market value but most importantly, houses that will cash flow. You'll learn how to locate people that are motivated to sell and sell quickly. They have their reasons, and you have yours, so everyone walks away with mutual benefits. If your mortgage is $1000 and you collect $2000 in rent, you are cash flowing. You just need to pay Property tax, insurance, and occasional maintenance. All of that will cost about $200 a month for a $200,000 house.

I'm not an accountant, but I can tell you that depreciation breaks will offset your taxes. Like other investments, if you decide you don't want the properties, later on, you can sell it for a profit.

Everyone with a job can do this, and if you do it long enough, you won't need your job. Who doesn't want financial freedom? Passive income is the way. Watch this! If you make at a minimum 10 deals in 10 years like the first one I mentioned, you'll generate about $8,000 a month forever, with little or no effort.

All associated bills are already factored in. If you do nothing but work for the next 10 years, you'll have no passive income, and if you get laid off and replaced by artificial intelligence, you're in trouble. I'm not a lawyer, but I can tell you that artificial intelligence cannot take away your passive income cash flow through real estate, but first, you must get it.

200k House Rental (Monthly)

Rent	2000
Property Tax	-100
Insurance	-100
Mortgage	-954
HOA	-42
Maintenance and Vacancy	-200
Depreciation	381
Monthly Profit and Cashflow	985

*Note: Dep based on 200K house -75K land = 125K over 27.5 years will be $381/month. Remaining numbers are hypothetical.

Many that lack understanding of the overall picture of real estate investing often ask, why rentals? For starters, it generates cash flow, and it comes in the form of passive income. Rental properties are also a great strategy for increasing net worth.

Other pros of renting include equity buildup and tax incentives. Keep in mind that every rental must produce positive cash flow, therefore, treat each as its own and rent your property for cash flow first and foremost.

Rentals build equity from mortgage payments and appreciation while getting depreciation breaks for tax purposes. That's twenty-seven and a half years of deductions. I don't know any other business quite like this. The increase in value while receiving tax incentives are magical to me.

Some of the guidelines to follow when renting are employment and income verification, credit check, criminal check, and renter's insurance. The benefits are 1031 exchange, tax breaks, the satisfaction of providing shelter, money with little or no effort, and wealth building makes income rental property a favorite for many investors.

It is extremely important that you have a choice of tenants and always require a deposit. I see it as compulsory to set up an auto draft for rent. You can even get bank and credit card as backups, and when there's an NSF in the bank account, then you can draft from the tenant's credit card. Be sure to check your local laws such as landlord and tenant acts for your county.

As you get multiple properties, have your personal assistant manage them so you can spend your time making more deals. Always announce upcoming rentals early. Long term rentals of single-family rental or SFR with great cash flow is the idea but you must pre-plan to avoid long vacancy period. The key is to announce an upcoming rental early.

Make it a policy to only lease 1 year minimum for long term and require a 30-day notice for move outs. Notify your rental list about newly renovated property by emailing and texting them. Place a house for rent yard sign in front of the house and Include the number of beds and bath. Add company name telephone.

The real estate agent can list and collect commission when the property is leased. They will put the property in front of a much larger audience.

Agents will show the property to prospective tenants. They will also handle the lease agreement.

The higher return on investment for single-family rentals is vacation rental using companies such as Trip Advisors and Airbnb and Homeaway.com. There are booking agents that will handle your listings and inquiries. These agents will manage and price the property correctly for maximum profits. They'll even coordinate maintenance and housekeeping.

Use booking agents to get your property rented out more efficiently. Most of them only charge 10% but screen them for the ones that stays mostly booked. You'll find more success with your newly renovated homes using these agents. Be sure to furnish the home well because it will help you keep the property booked at all times.

Entry strategy for rental business should be multi-units whenever possible. Residential real estate is classified as any single-family property from 1 to 4 units.

Any more than that is considered commercial. If you don't own a home, maximize your entry by buying the maximum units in residential and renting them for passive income. You must qualify anyway to buy your first home, so this strategy gives you a grand style entry.

Some states may require that you live there for at least a year. This is a small price to pay for the benefits I'm about to disclose. The best way to sustain and grow in this real estate business is to use other people's money or OPM. This can be achieved through lending.

Down payment can become a problem, so you want to use your money as efficiently as possible. The problem is that lenders will require a 10% to 15% down payment on the sale price plus you'll have another 3% expense in closing cost. This is standard for investment properties. However, the technique I want you to use will get you the biggest bang for your bucks. You get plenty for spending the least amount.

When you take the "my first home" approach, you'll only require a 3% down payment as opposed to 10% to 15% for regular investors. You can attain this 3% down payment through conventional or FHA loans. Remember that you are using other people money as much as possible so saving money in down payment means having more money to do your next deal which will no longer be considered first time home but rather an investment.

As I mentioned, that carries up to 15% down payment for your first one to four stand-alone properties. Your next 5 to 10 properties will require an even greater down payment. Currently, I see 20% to 25% down as the standards for this number of properties. I explained all of this to show you that a maximum mindset should be your approach.

Now back to your first home, there are special programs that will allow you a zero-down payment. One such program is called acorn first time home buyer, but there are more. Imagine being able to secure a four-plex with no money down and only 3% in closing cost, how great would that be?

You can rent the other 3 units and even rent the fourth units after 1 year if that's what your lender stipulates. Now you have the other 3 tenants paying the mortgage for you with extra money left as passive income to be re-invested into your next deal. You need to give yourself at least 1 year for a rental property to stabilize.

When you locate a property, make sure you perform due diligence to avoid flood zones and war zones. Rental property primary focus should be cash flow but get the ones with equity. Other benefits, such as equity increase and depreciation, are bonuses.

Every landlord should have at their disposal a rental agreement and eviction preparation carefully crafted by an experienced attorney. Do not feel tempted to use a generic form because there are local laws that landlords must follow. The only sure way to comply is by having your lawyer who specializes in residential real estate lease in your area to do it. A rental property should be local only when you first start the business. This strategy will enable you to visit once or twice a year to check the condition of the property.

Remember that you always have a choice when it comes to leasing your property to a tenant. If the person does not qualify, denial them and lease to one that does, second-guessing your processes can come back and bite you later. Every new tenant should be required to pay a deposit. A preferred way should be to set up an auto draft for rent by getting bank and credit card information as well as permission with signature to do so. In the event there's NSF in a bank account, the credit card is immediately charged.

As a landlord, you must be familiar with your local laws. For instance, serious rental income owners should know any landlord and tenant acts for their county. Although you can start out managing your own rentals in the beginning, plan on delegating that responsibility to your personal assistance once you get more properties under your control.

CHAPTER 14

ALTERNATIVE SEARCHES FOR PROPERTIES

When searching for foreclosures, you can still start by look for those that are not listed in the MLS. By now, you know my methods of identifying properties are opposite of what the majority are doing. There's less competition, so this is a great way to find better and below market deals. Smaller banks tend not to list their foreclosures, so put more focus on these banks. They may also have REO or Real Estate Owned properties, which are a result of failed sale during a foreclosure. Well, the bank's business is not real estate so they are willing to sell as fast as they get them.

Although my methodology of finding great deals in real estate is through direct marketing where you identify motivated sellers or smaller banks, most tourism and vacation areas have a bit of scarcity. It doesn't mean you won't find distressed sellers or REO's, but it may be challenging. The remedy is to use additional methods such as MLS, Foreclosures, and Short sales.

Although these properties are typically listed, I'll show you strategies to still find deals below market value. One technique is to focus strictly on listings that are older than 120 days on the MLS. Once you get access to the MLS, you can set reminders to automatically get notified through email when a property reaches this threshold. At this point, the deal is no longer attractive to buyers; therefore, the owner is now willing to negotiate and sell. The banks usually have a percentage that they can accept. Talking to other investors in your local market can reveal what the percentage may be since the banks themselves will not tell you.

While driving about your daily business routines, you'll see a lot of for sale by owner signs. Simply take a picture of the sign and research the property to see and if it has potential, call the seller and proceed to ask the questions on the lead intake form. Upon completion, do a desktop evaluation and if you determine that the seller is motivated based on the answers and asking price, go ahead and do a site evaluation using the repair estimate form to see if there's enough room to meet your desired number. If so, make an offer and get the property under contract so you can begin your due diligence.

Going to your county courthouse every couple of months for the eviction records will give you access to landlords that may be fed up and ready to sell. Indeed, a series of bad tenants can cause a seller to be motivated. As far as I'm concerned, a landlord that is knowledgeable and experienced should not have bad tenants after bad tenants. The screening process should eliminate that. This means you can buy the property and use the correct approach to avoid such mistakes.

A failing business for one person doesn't mean the same for you. If anything at all, it will teach you what mistakes to stir clear of. With the fundamental strategies you learn here and the exercise of looking at and doing deals, you'll be at a much better position to succeed than those that lack the knowledge and experience.

Other alternative searches such as tax lien, MLS through real estate agents, yard signs, direct mail, foreclosures, social media, and craigslist can all be utilized to capture leads. When these leads are properly managed, many will become prospects, and some will ultimately turn into sellers. It's a numbers game, so the more leads you get, the greater your chance of doing deals.

Anytime a lender takes back their property, and the market value is less than what is owed, it is a candidate for a short sale. Please understand that an appraisal is different from market value. Even if the property is appraised at a certain amount, the market value can vary because it is based on what people are paying at a particular moment in a specific area on similar properties. This is why sales comparable is so powerful in determining apples to apples in pricing.

CHAPTER 15

SEEK TO MAXIMIZE YOUR INVESTMENTS

Although there's much success in single-family rentals, I tend to prefer the multi-family rentals over it because it provides benefits I can't overlook. This and many other wisdoms didn't occur overnight. It took the experience of trial and error over the years for me to fine-tune my real estate investor acumen. Although my attitude towards learning is that it should never stop, I'm very comfortable with the execution of my real estate approach.

When I began developing homes in 2005, I did not know these types of strategies. I knew how to get builders and general contractors to get the job done, but the tricks of the trade developed throughout the years. As the projects continued, however, I learned more, and today I'm in a position to help you avoid some of the pitfalls I endured. Throughout this publication, I will drop gems that will forward your agenda in building wealth with real estate.

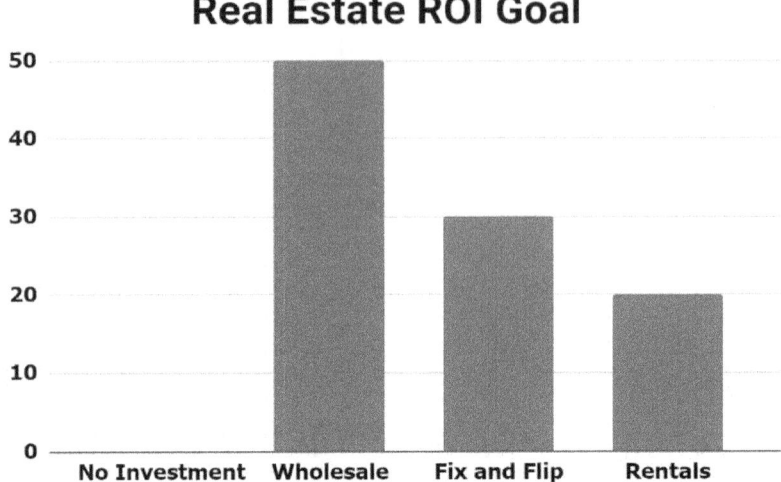

Whenever possible, rent multifamily units such as duplex, triplex, and fourplex. Since you have multiple units on the same property, they will require less work on maintenance and property management. If one tenant moves out, you still have the others. These multifamily rentals have a higher return on investment or ROI as a result of someone always there to pay rent. A vacancy in a single-family rental means zero income, but with duplex, for example, you still have the other tenant. A four-plex in the same scenario of 1 vacancy would not suffer a great loss since three other tenants are still paying rent.

Even during the rehab stage, one building with multiple units means one roof, one floor, one yard, and one place to renovate. There's no need for multiple contractors on this project. When it's time for inspection, you only have to do it one time. The revenue that is generated may be the same, but the expenses are less with multi-family units.

Residential real estate is classified as any single-family property from 1 to four units. Any more than that is considered commercial. If you don't own a home, maximize your entry by buying the maximum units in residential and renting them for passive income. You must qualify anyway to buy your first home, so this strategy gives you a grand style entry

Some states may require that you live there for at least a year. This is a small price to pay for the benefits I'm about to disclose. The best way to do sustain and grow in this business. All real estate business is to use other people's money or OPM. This can be achieved through lenders and other investors. The problem is that lenders will require a 10% to 15% down payment ongoing the sale price plus you'll have another 3% expense in closing cost. This is standard for the business itself however the technique I want you to use will get you the biggest bang for your bucks. You're get plenty for spending the least amount.

When you take the "my first home" approach, you'll only be required a 3% down payment as opposed to 10% to 15% for regular investors. You can attain this 3% down payment through conventional or FHA loans. Remember that you are using other people money as much as possible so saving money in down payment means having more money to do your next deal which will no longer be considered first time home but rather an investment.

As I mentioned, that carries an up to 15% down payment for your first one to four stand-alone properties. Your next 5 to 10 properties will require an even greater down payment. Currently I see 20% to 25% down as the standards for this number of properties. I explained all of this to show you that a maximum mindset should be your approach.

Now back to your first home, there are special programs that will allow you a zero-down payment. One such program is called acorn first time home buyer but there are more. Imagine being able to secure a four-plex with no money down and only 3% in closing cost, how great would that be? You can rent the other 3 units and even rent the fourth units after 1 year if that's what your lender stipulates. Now you have the other 3 tenants paying the mortgage for you with extra money left as passive income to be re-invested into your next deal.

The higher return on investment for a single-family rental is vacation rental such as Trip Advisors and Airbnb and Homeaway.com. There are booking agents that will handle your listings and inquiries. These agents will manage and price the property correctly for maximum profits. They'll even coordinate maintenance and housekeeping. Most of them only charge 10%. You'll find success with your newly renovated homes. Be sure to furnish the home well because it will help you keep the property booked at all times.

When to locate property, make sure you perform due diligence to avoid flood zones and war zones. Rental property primary focus should be cash flow. Other benefits such as equity increase and depreciation are bonuses. Keep increasing seller lead to make more deals. You need to give yourself at least 1 year for rental property to stabilize

When you place your house on the market, you must require pre-approval letter from your lender and non-refundable earnest money before accepting an offer. After inspection, give buyer extra money to fix any major things that must be repaired for the deal to go forward. Close the deal without wasting any more time.

When I began developing homes in 2005, I knew not these types of strategies. I just knew how to get builders and general contractors to get the job done. As the projects continued however, I learned more and today I'm in a position to help you avoid some of the pitfalls I endured. Throughout this publication, I have dropped gems that will forward your agenda in building wealth with real estate.

Rent multifamily such as duplex, triplex, and four plex as much as possible. Since you have multiple units on the same property, you'll work less on maintain the property. If one tenant moves out, you still have the others. These multifamily has a higher return on investment or ROI.

CHAPTER 16

VIABLE RENTAL WITH HIGH ROI

Other than the traditional rentals which are great, there are others that can generate even greater ROI. These rental types cost more, but the earning potential also increases significantly.

The one I want to focus on is vacation rentals. This type of rental is a short term of less than 1 month at a time. It is usually rented for a few days, weekly or a few weeks but less than a month.

I emphasize less than a month because there are local ordinances that govern short term rental. You may also need a license to operate as well as hotel occupancy tax.

The key is to do independent research in your area to see what requirements apply. The earning potential is definitely worth the research.

The premise of effective and efficient short-term rentals is utilizing a booking agent with a track record of success. Companies like VRBO, Homeaway.com, Trip Advisors, and Airbnb provides excellent service in listing and booking rentals. Of course, comfortability and appearance are huge therefore take that into consideration when you furnish the rental. Since your property is a newly renovated, that part of the vanity is already covered. Photos and videos of the property and its amenities are what keep rentals booked so go the extra mile and make it nice.

You'll have to adequately entice people into wanting to book your rental by making it appealing with details such as access to internet connection, washer/dryer, cable TV and especially the number of beds, etc. Those that cut corners with their rental won't be as successful because there are other choices for customers. You also want great reviews, so it's important to keep things such as landscaping and cleanliness a top priority.

Yes, you'll have additional expenses in this style of rentals such as utilities, lawn care, housekeeping, booking fees, and occupancy taxes however if your rental stays occupied and is priced correctly, you'll still earn a high return on investment.

Student housing is another one that can generate greater returns because you can rent it by the room. Imagine being able to rent a 3-bedroom house to 3 tenants. You'll make more money than renting it all to one family. Parents should be required to co-sign, so there's a security factor of being certain that if students are unable to pay, parents will. The only requirement is that you buy a rental income property near a college or university.

It doesn't have to be limited to the largest universities only. There are hundreds of smaller colleges all over that can be explored. Research your area of interest to see what opportunities exist because many college students prefer to live off campus even when there's availability on campus for room and boarding. It's about identifying a need for student housing and fulfilling it for cash flow.

You should also be aware that students will be students, so when you decide to rent to them, take measures during the rehab stages to use strong and durable materials.

This is more so with student housing than any other group. An action such as laminate floor versus carpet and stronger countertop like granite versus formica are just a couple of examples to consider. Stronger doors and heavy-duty bathroom and kitchen appliances will also help minimize your maintenance cost.

The option of providing furniture or not is a matter of what other landlords in your area are doing. You want to be competitive, so if furniture is included for student housing, you'll have to do the same.

The approach to furnishings should be opposite to that of construction and rehab. Don't spend a lot of money buying the most expensive furniture. A good durable second hand will suffice.

Either vacation rentals or student housing are both strategies that can produce a higher return on investment than traditional leasing; however, you must run your business well. Again, two people can engage in a nearly identical business, and one will fail miserably while the other flourish with success. The outcome is not luck. Its strategies and how it is applied. The correct application of the strategies outlined here will put you closer to achieving your goal.

CONCLUSION

Deep knowledge of fundamental strategies and creativity is a great combination for building wealth with real estate. It's about leveraging what you know with other people resources, money, skills, and experience to produce ongoing profits. A level of commitment is required for those that want to make it in the business of real estate. Most importantly, you must always look to help others before thinking of what's in for you.

Being of service to others has been my policy since I was a young adult. As a result, business transactions tend to follow in many cases. Years ago, prior to mentoring people in business and real estate, I would volunteer my assistance in helping my friends & family get out of debt and build great credit. Through word of mouth, others reached out to me. It was all organic, although I would later take heed to establish avenues to reach to the masses. A simple gesture of a helping hand has enabled me to generate revenue.

In the world of real estate investing, you come across a lot of distress homeowners that are motivated to sell for all type of reasons. Treat them with respect and dignity. Listen to their problem and create a solution for them. In the process, your real estate business will benefit. Many think of wholesaling properties as taking advantage of an unfortunate situation. For me, that is farthest from the truth. When I search for motivated sellers, my primary purpose is to identify the cause of distress and propose a solution.

Life caused the distress condition for the seller, and you are only there to rescue them. If not you, someone else will reach out or often at times, what seemed bad for the homeowner could only get worse if some positive action is not taken. Both parties know this, and that's why a reasonable offer with all things factored in is usually accepted. A number of those that reject the first offer will make a counteroffer. If the numbers make sense, you can accept. It's about being able to help and make a profit for your business.

All the fundamental strategies discussed in this book is evergreen. This means that you can apply it now and years to come to make money in real estate. As you begin to establish your business, keep in mind that you need a community of like-minded people and mentorship. You can have FREE access to this support by joining my Facebook master group. It's called Devise wealth Mastermind, and you'll find additional resources there to help you.

Much success to you!

OTHER PUBLICATIONS
BY KENNETH BOTWE

PURSUIT OF ~~HAPPINESS~~ ASSETS

LITTLE MONEY BIG CREDIT

5 PRINCIPLES FOR BECOMING WEALTHY

NURTURE